the gluten-free
kitchen

THE GLUTEN-FREE KITCHEN

An Hachette UK Company
www.hachette.co.uk

Vie Books, an imprint of Summersdale Publishers
Part of Octopus Publishing Group Limited
Carmelite House
50 Victoria Embankment
LONDON
EC4Y 0DZ
UK

www.summersdale.com

Printed and bound in China

ISBN: 978-1-83799-299-7

Substantial discounts on bulk quantities of Summersdale books are available to corporations, professional associations and other organizations. For details contact general enquiries: telephone: +44 (0) 1243 771107 or email: enquiries@summersdale.com.

Neither the author nor the publisher can be held responsible for any injury, loss or claim – be it health, financial or otherwise – arising out of the use, or misuse, of the suggestions made herein. Always consult your doctor before trying any new diet if you have a medical or health condition, or are worried about any of the side effects. This book is not intended as a substitute for the medical advice of a doctor or physician.

the gluten-free kitchen

SIMPLE IDEAS AND DELICIOUS, NUTRITIOUS RECIPES TO HELP YOU LIVE GLUTEN-FREE

EMILY KERRIGAN

For Chloe

Contents

Introduction

Being diagnosed as coeliac or advised to follow a gluten-free diet can feel overwhelming and confusing. You'll probably feel pretty gloomy initially, thinking you can't eat freshly baked bread or your favourite slice of pizza anymore. Well stop fretting – this book is here to help.

About one in a hundred people worldwide have coeliac disease and more than half a million more in the UK may have unexplained symptoms. So you are definitely not alone. If you're reading this, you may well be at the start of your gluten-free journey, in which case you're probably wondering how you will ever enjoy dinner out again, and whether you need to buy a new toaster (spoiler alert: you do). Or perhaps you've been at the gluten-free game for a while and you're simply looking for some tasty new ideas for lunch (p.42), a foolproof sandwich loaf recipe (p.112) or a brilliant cake for your coeliac child's sixth birthday (p.136). Either way, this book is for you.

Now get ready to smile. The best thing about being gluten-free is all the delicious food you get to cook from scratch. The gluten-free lifestyle needn't feel like a punishment. Flip this idea on its head and instead, think that you've been invited to an exclusive party where you get to try fresh, new flavours and ingredients. You need never settle for sad, sweaty sandwiches

wrapped in cellophane again. Instead, your body has given you the best excuse to prioritize cooking with fresh produce, herbs, spices and other naturally gluten-free ingredients, while boosting your health and avoiding gluten-containing junk foods that can be high in salt, sugar and fat.

This book walks you through setting up your delicious, new gluten-free kitchen. It lists all the ingredients you can continue to use and those you must avoid, alongside particular nutrients you should ensure you get plenty of. It also offers handy tips on meal-planning, keeping costs down and how cooking gluten-free from scratch can save you money. You will find 59 delicious, easy and nutritious recipe ideas for breakfast, lunch, snacks and dinner, as well as gluten-free baking (because in a balanced gluten-free diet, chocolate still has its place). And yes, these recipes do also include brilliant freshly baked bread (p.112, p.114) and pizza (p.84) so you definitely don't need to feel glum.

So what are you waiting for? Let's get in the kitchen and start cooking gluten-free.

» PART ONE:

How to make your kitchen gluten-free

What is coeliac disease?

Coeliac disease is a lifelong autoimmune disease which causes an inflammatory response in the gut, reducing absorption of nutrients from food. Our small intestines are lined with numerous tiny, finger-like projections called villi which increase the surface area of the gut to maximize absorption of key nutrients from the food we eat. In coeliac disease, when gluten comes into contact with these villi, the immune system triggers a response, attacking them as "foreign". This damages the villi causing bloating, diarrhoea and/or constipation, nausea and vomiting, gas, abdominal pain, fatigue, possible weight loss, and poor growth in children. The associated malabsorption often leads to anaemia, due to a lack of iron or folate, alongside calcium deficiency, which may affect bone mineral density, weaken tooth enamel and increase the risk of fractures or osteoporosis. Other symptoms can include unexplained subfertility, mouth ulcers and an itchy skin rash called *Dermatitis herpetiformis*. Not all coeliacs suffer all symptoms, and the charity Coeliac UK lists all possible symptoms in detail, including serious complications. If you suspect you may be coeliac, speak to your doctor who can confirm a diagnosis with a simple blood test, followed by an intestinal biopsy (often not necessary in children). It's very important you don't eliminate gluten from your diet until you have had the test – even for a few days – as otherwise, you may get a false negative.

How is it treated?

Currently, the treatment for coeliac disease is lifelong avoidance of gluten, the protein found in wheat, barley and rye. Most people can tolerate uncontaminated oats but some may also need to avoid these. Even the tiniest crumb of gluten is harmful for coeliacs, but the good news is that with strict adherence to a gluten-free diet, your gut will heal, your symptoms will resolve and your risk of complications such as osteoporosis will lower. Above all, don't panic. Focus on recovering, get stuck into learning some new recipes and concentrate on the foods that you can eat, not those you can't.

Getting calcium and iron, and enjoying a balanced diet

If you have recently been diagnosed with coeliac disease it's important you focus on eating a balanced diet; high in vegetables, fruits, wholegrains, omega-3s and healthy fats while low in saturated fat, sugar and salt. As your gut begins to heal, you will soon feel the benefit of giving your body the key nutrients it needs to thrive. It's particularly necessary to ensure you're getting enough calcium and iron. Studies show that up to 75 per cent of those with coeliac disease suffer from low bone mineral density at diagnosis, while 30–50 per cent of those recently diagnosed have iron-deficiency anaemia. Calcium-rich foods include milk, cheese, yoghurt, leafy green vegetables and fish where you eat the bones, like sardines or anchovies. Red meat, beans such as edamame or chickpeas, egg yolks, lentils, tahini, oats, nuts and dried apricots are all good sources of iron. The recipes in this book are nutrient-dense and focus on a rainbow of veg, wholegrains, omega-3s and healthy fats. The baking section does include some high-in-sugar and saturated-fat recipes, such as a chocolate cake perfect for birthday parties. Enjoy these recipes occasionally as part of a balanced diet. You'll also find healthier baking options in the book too, such as lower-sugar granola (p.34), carrot cake frosting (p.132) and American-style pancakes (p.36).

What about non-coeliac gluten sensitivity or wheat allergy?

While non-coeliac sensitivity (including gluten intolerance) is a bit of a grey area research-wise, many non-coeliacs find that eliminating gluten from their diets alleviates any digestive niggles they are experiencing. There are no rules, and you know your body best – if you are not coeliac, you may be intolerant and simply find you feel better without gluten. If you do have a coeliac test, it's very important you don't eliminate gluten from your diet – even for a few days – because you may get a false negative. If the result rules out coeliac disease, and if other causes of your symptoms have also been ruled out, speak to your healthcare team. You may jointly decide that following a gluten-free diet is best for you. A wheat allergy is not the same as coeliac disease but rather an allergic response triggered by eating wheat which develops within seconds or minutes and causes swelling or itching of the mouth, hives or a rash, wheezing or coughing.

Ingredients you can still enjoy

The following foods are all naturally gluten-free:

- Beans and pulses
- Dairy products: milk, cream, cheese, natural and Greek yoghurt
- Eggs
- Fresh fish and shellfish
- Fresh poultry and meat
- Fresh yeast
- Fruit and veg
- Herbs and spices
- Oils such as olive, vegetable, sesame and sunflower
- Plain nuts and seeds
- Plain unmarinated tofu
- Polenta and corn
- Potatoes
- Quinoa and buckwheat
- Rice and rice noodles
- Sugar, honey and vanilla extract

See the A–Z of ingredients on p.21 for popular gluten-free alternative ingredients.

Foods and ingredients to avoid

The charity Coeliac UK carries a complete downloadable checklist of gluten-containing ingredients and gluten-free alternatives on its website (www.coeliac.org.uk). As an overview, the following are not gluten-free:

>> WHEAT, RYE OR BARLEY AND THEIR FLOURS

- Bulgur, couscous, durum, farro, freekeh, kamut, pearl barley, rye, semolina, spelt

>> BATTERED/ BREADCRUMBED/ COATED IN FLOUR

- Fish or shellfish
- Meat and poultry
- Potatoes
- Vegetables

>> DRINKS

- Ales, beers, lagers and stouts
- Barley waters and squash
- Malted milk drinks

>> READY-MADE

- Biscuits, breads, cakes, chapattis, crackers, muffins, pastries and pizza bases
- Breadsticks, pretzels and many snacks
- Ice cream cones and wafers, liquorice sweets, puddings
- Muesli, wheat-based breakfast cereals

>> COMMON INGREDIENTS

- Canned, dried and fresh wheat noodles and pasta
- Most soy sauces
- Porridge oats, oat milk, oat-based snacks that are not labelled gluten-free

Hidden gluten

Check the label of anything that comes in a packet. Even ingredients you know to be naturally gluten-free, such as lentils, may carry a warning that they've been processed in a factory that handles wheat. In the UK, US and Australia, gluten-containing or possibly contaminated products must be labelled as such. Coeliac UK also has a brilliant (paid-for) smartphone app which scans the barcode of thousands of supermarket products to give you an instant answer on this as you shop.

Beware, in particular, of thickeners, stocks and stock cubes, gravy, sauces and fried foods. Other products that you may not necessarily think of as gluten-containing but which are (or often are) include: some sausages, burgers and cured meats such as salami, taramasalata, Worcestershire sauce, some chocolate, some meringues, some flavoured yoghurts and ice creams, Marmite, confectionery, potato croquettes, dry-roasted nuts, some packets of grated cheese, some crisps and popcorn, some mustards and vinegars, some peanut butters and dips, malted milk drinks, cake decorations like sprinkles – the list goes on.

In short, always check the label and if in doubt, avoid.

Decontaminating your kitchen

The safest kitchen for a coeliac is an entirely gluten-free one. First up, you'll need to deep clean your kitchen and all its contents to rid it of all traces of gluten. Go through your kitchen cupboards removing gluten-containing foods and donate unopened packets/cans to a food bank. You'll need a new toaster and to replace pastry brushes, wooden spoons, rolling pins and chopping boards… if in doubt, throw it out and replace to create a fail-safe, gluten-free zone.

If you don't live alone and some of you are planning to continue eating gluten, you'll need to keep gluten-free food and cooking kit separate. Metallic and plastic equipment can be cleaned thoroughly between uses, but you should try to have two of everything else, designated as gluten-free by marking the handles. Label coeliac-only foods to avoid mix-ups. For example, you will need coeliac-only butter stored separately to avoid cross-contamination from a knife used to butter standard toast.

Invest in Tupperware, tins and jars to protect gluten-free goods and store them well away from gluten-containing equivalents. Use a clean grill pan, separate toaster or toaster bags for gluten-free toast – remind everyone that even a crumb of gluten is harmful for a coeliac. That means no frying gluten-free food in oil used for gluten-containing foods. And if you're making bread or pizza dough, be especially careful to avoid cross-contaminating gluten-free dough with ordinary gluten-containing flour scattered across a floury worktop. Airborne flour gets everywhere – don't let it near food being prepared for a coeliac. Needless to say, eating out or at your family and friends' houses is going to need forward planning and due consideration now, too.

Gluten-free swaps, standbys and SOS snacks

›› THREE EASY SWAPS

- Konjac noodles are good substitutes for egg noodles (see p.70).
- Little lettuce leaf cups make emergency replacements for pitta breads or burger buns.
- Quinoa, buckwheat or canned lentils can replace couscous in salads (see p.50, p.54 and p.76).

›› THREE EMERGENCY STANDBYS

- Frozen gluten-free tortilla wraps defrost instantly on a hot griddle for filled wraps (see p.46) or fajitas.
- Rice noodles can form the basis of quick noodle salads (see p.48) or Summer rolls (see p.52).
- Rice pouches in cupboards can become instant fried rice (see p.82).

›› THREE EMERGENCY SNACKS

If you are caught unprepared most grocery stores and supermarkets will stock popcorn, rice cakes or oat cakes which can all be coeliac-friendly. But always check the label as some oats, or bags of popcorn, are processed in factories that handle wheat. And remember to keep a well-stocked fruit bowl.

Use this book to help you plan

Whether you want to make some food ahead of time, stock your freezer or cupboard, make a meal in 15 minutes or less, or cook tonight with supermarket-sweep ingredients you've grabbed quickly on the way home, this book has you covered.

►► READY IN 15 MINUTES OR LESS

- Nut butter, blueberry and banana toast
- Breakfast smoothies
- Buckwheat and oat cinnamon porridge
- American-style banana pancakes
- Traditional pancakes
- Houmous jam jar dip
- Chicken and avocado wrap
- Rainbow noodle salad
- Halloumi burger
- Extra green pesto pasta
- Veggie fried rice
- Sushi poke bowls
- Nachos
- Smoked salmon hotcakes
- Pasta puttanesca
- Garlic bread
- Easy cheesecake pots
- Chocolate brownie bites

►► SUPERMARKET-SWEEP MEALS

- Houmous jam jar dip
- Chicken and avocado wrap
- Rainbow noodle salad
- Halloumi burger
- Salmon with greens and grains
- Pinwheel salads
- Fishfinger sandwich
- Extra green pesto pasta
- Nachos
- Cheat's tomato risotto
- Cheat's chicken tikka
- Storecupboard smoky bean stew
- Kedgeree
- Smoked salmon hotcakes
- Sushi poke bowls

>> MAKE AHEAD

- Houmous jam jar dip
- Rainbow noodle salad
- Rainbow veggie bowl
- Edamame falafel with tabbouleh
- Chicken and rice soup
- Pinwheel salads
- Pasta veggienese
- Granola
- Chocolate brownie bites
- Chocolate gingernut bark
- Breakfast smoothies

>> FREEZABLE

- Sweet potato soup
- Chicken and rice soup
- Extra green pesto
- Pasta veggienese
- Easy white loaf
- Seeded oat bread
- Cornbread
- Garlic bread
- Pizza muffins
- Gingernut biscuits
- Frozen cookie dough
- Ice cream waffle sandwiches

>> USES CUPBOARD STAPLES

- Buckwheat and oat cinnamon porridge
- Granola
- Houmous jam jar dip
- Salmon with greens and grains
- Veggie fried rice
- Lentil polpette
- Cheat's paella
- Chicken tikka kebabs
- Pasta puttanesca
- Storecupboard smoky bean stew

TOP 5 RECOMMENDED BITS OF KITCHEN KIT
FOR THE RECIPES IN THIS BOOK

Digital scales for accurate weighing – really important!

Food processor for chopping ingredients and mixing dough

Handheld electric beaters for whisking cake batters and frostings

Silicone spatula to get every last bit of batter out of the bowl

Julienne peeler to grate carrots like a pro

Saving money

Unfortunately, ready-made gluten-free foods and bags of pasta and flour are more expensive at the supermarket. The good news is that gluten-free needn't always cost more if you learn to plan and prep your meals from home (see pp.18–19). In fact, if you consider how quickly convenience foods add up over a typical day versus preparing your own food, you can actually save money each day – not to mention doing your bit for the planet by cutting down on throwaway packaging. Below are some tips to save money and cut food waste:

- Make a weekly meal plan and shopping list, taking stock of the ingredients currently in your cupboards.
- Buy long-lasting dry goods like gluten-free pasta, noodles and oats, polenta and rice in bulk.
- Use frozen fruit and veg which are affordable, convenient and just as nutritious.
- Turn the ends of loaves into breadcrumbs then freeze to coat foods you prep at home, such as the fishfingers on p.78 or Arancini on p.102.
- Batch cook meals to store in your freezer, such as the soups on p.64 and p.96 or cookies on p.140.
- Use up leftover vegetables in recipes like the Rainbow veggie bowl on p.54 or Veggie fried rice on p.82.

PART TWO

The A–Z of gluten-free ingredients

Ingredients

Many of the recipes in this book use day-to-day ingredients or staples available in any supermarket, which just happen to be gluten-free, such as ground almonds, lentils or rice noodles. Where gluten-free flours are listed, these generally refer to readily available Doves Farm "Freee" flours which are blends of rice, potato, tapioca, maize and buckwheat flours. By using these or similar blends, you may negate the need to invest in individual bags of different flours, thus cutting costs. Having said that, part of the fun of a gluten-free kitchen comes in experimenting with different ingredients. Below is a list of staples, together with one or two specific ingredients you will come across as you read more widely about gluten-free cookery.

» ALMOND FLOUR

Ground almonds and almond meal are the same ingredient by two names. Almond flour is ground almonds, only with the almond skins removed which makes it finer. It is a staple in gluten-free cakes and may also be used as a substitute for breadcrumbs in savoury recipes. Try in a Lemon drizzle cake (p.134) or to bind together Lentil polpette (p.90).

» BAKING POWDER

Beware that some shop-bought baking powders are made with wheat starch or wheat flour, so ensure you buy gluten-free versions.

⟫ BUCKWHEAT

Despite the name, buckwheat is a gluten-free grain and can be used like quinoa in salads (p.50, p.54) or to add extra bite to a bowl of porridge (p.32). You might see buckwheat bread flour at the supermarket but check the label as some brands are processed in factories handling wheat.

⟫ COCONUT FLOUR

Made from finely ground, dried coconut flesh and mildly sweet tasting, coconut flour is great for baking or thickening curries.

⟫ GRAM FLOUR

Also known as chickpea flour, this is a staple in Asian cookery for use in savoury pancakes. Try it in place of cornflour in the corn hotcakes on p.95.

⟫ KONJAC (OR SHIRATAKI) NOODLES

Konjac flour, derived from yams grown in Asia, is the basis for these chunky shirataki noodles which are ideal gluten-free substitutes for wheat-containing egg noodles. They are sold wok-ready in packs and need no pre-cooking, plus they hold their shape in the pan when stir-fried. Watch the label as some include gluten-containing oats, others not. Try in Japanese noodles (p.70).

⟫ MILLET FLOUR

An ancient grain which gives cakes and muffins a good, not-too-crumbly texture. You might see it on the label of packaged gluten-free goods. If you want to try baking with it, look for it in Asian grocers and health food shops.

>> OATS

The majority of coeliacs can tolerate certified gluten-free oats although be aware that some are sensitive to avenin, a protein found in oats.

>> POLENTA

Try baking with this in a Lemon drizzle cake (p.134) or use like flour in hotcakes (p.95).

>> PSYLLIUM HUSK POWDER

When combined with water, the husks of psyllium seeds create a gel that stabilizes gluten-free dough, giving it a texture similar to standard bread. It's not cheap but a little goes a long way in bread-baking recipes if you want to try it. You'll also see it on the label of packaged gluten-free goods.

>> QUINOA

A complete plant protein and quick-to-cook grain that can be used in salads (p.54), Tabbouleh (p.50) and mixed with rice in hot dishes (p.98). Quinoa flour can be used in bread making and has a strong, almost grassy-like flavour.

>> RICE FLOUR AND NOODLES

Brown rice flour makes a good gluten-free sourdough starter to experiment with (try it too in the Little carrot cakes on p.132). Try white rice flour in the cookie dough on p.140. Vermicelli rice noodles have the advantage of cooking quickly and are perfect in Summer rolls (p.52). Avoid using in stir-fries as they disintegrate. Flat rice noodles are best for pad Thai or noodle salads (p.48).

SORGHUM FLOUR

A mildly sweet flavour makes sorghum a good bet to try in biscuits and cakes. Look for it in health food shops.

TAMARI

Gluten-free Japanese soy sauce. Try in Veggie fried rice (p.82) or Japanese noodles (p.70).

XANTHAN GUM

An emulsifier that helps gluten-free bread to bind in the same way as standard bread. Try it in Focaccia (p.120), Pretzels (p.122) or Banana bread (p.126). Some people with gluten intolerance can be sensitive to xanthan gum so bear this in mind if you notice any sensitivity after baking with it.

YEAST

Be aware that fresh yeast from a bakery may likely be contaminated – packaged gluten-free dried yeast is a safe bet.

» PART THREE:

Recipes

Glossary

The recipes in this book are easy enough for beginner cooks, but you might want to refer to the glossary of cooking terms below:

- **Cream (method)** – Beat together with electric beaters until pale and fluffy.
- **Diced** – Chop into small cubes (a dice) with a sharp knife.
- **Julienne** – Slice into very thin strips (a handheld julienne peeler does this for you in seconds).
- **Marble** – Partially stir one mixture into another leaving a ripple effect (using a knife or thin object).
- **Pulse/blitz or whizz** – Use a food processor on a pulse/automatic setting.
- **Season** – Add salt and/or pepper to taste.
- **Soft, medium and stiff peaks** – Whip cream to three different thicknesses depending on how long it is beaten.
- **Sweat** – Cook (typically onions and other veg) gently in a little oil until it begins to soften.
- **Whisk** – Beat air into a mixture with a fork, or a balloon whisk if the recipe specifies this.

BREAKFAST

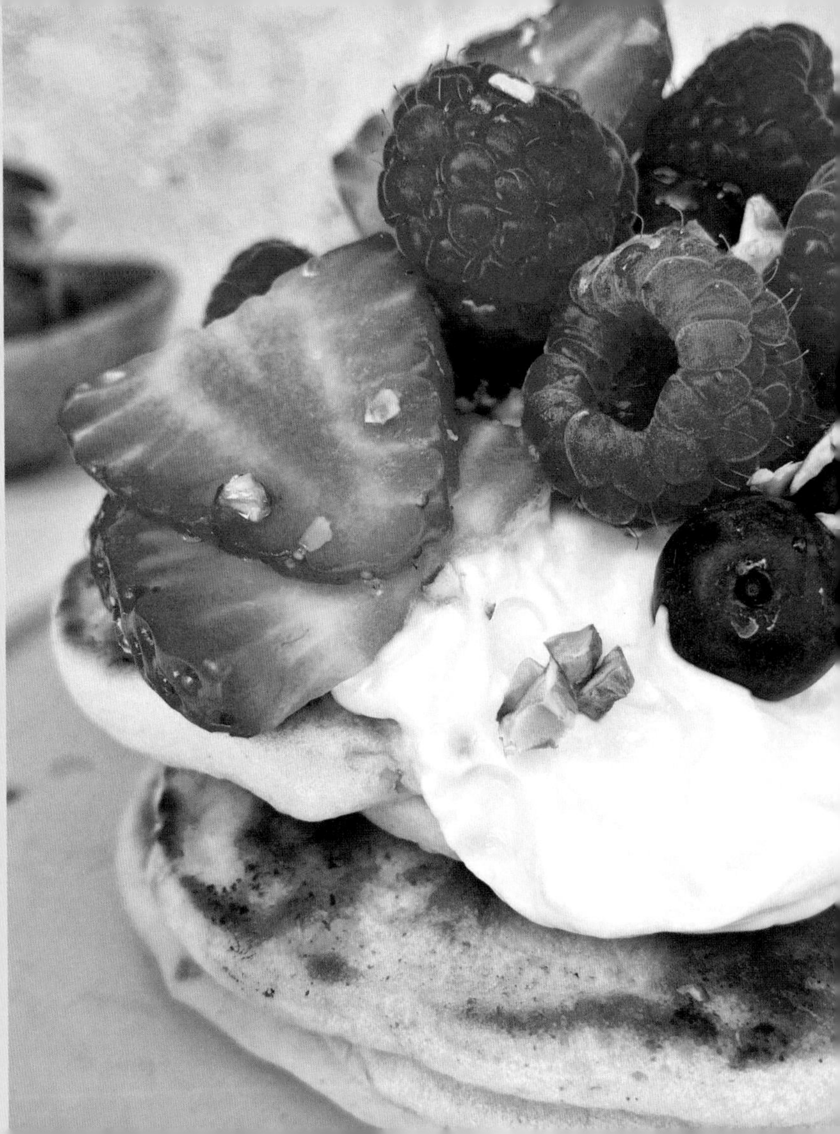

Nut butter, blueberry and banana toast

Batch cook and freeze Seeded oat bread (p.114) ready sliced. That way you always have a stash to toast straight from frozen when you want to use it in this nutritious, satisfying breakfast.

Serves 1 | Takes 5 minutes

INGREDIENTS

a slice of Seeded oat
  bread, toasted
gluten-free nut butter
1 banana, sliced
2 walnuts or pecans, chopped
a drizzle of honey or maple syrup
a handful of blueberries

METHOD

Spread the toast with a little nut butter then cover with the banana, chopped nuts, a drizzle of honey or maple syrup and a few blueberries. Slice in half with a sharp knife and serve.

Buckwheat and oat cinnamon porridge

Buckwheat isn't just for savoury gluten-free dishes like the salads on p.50 and p.54. If you have some in your cupboard, try adding it to your morning porridge to add a little nutritious texture and bite.

Serves 1 | Takes 10 minutes plus overnight soaking

INGREDIENTS

1 tbsp buckwheat
40 g (1½ oz) gluten-free oats
a pinch of cinnamon
250 ml (9 fl oz) milk
a handful of pumpkin seeds
a handful of strawberries
  and blueberries
mint (optional)

METHOD

Soak the buckwheat at room temperature overnight in a glass full of water to soften. Drain, then add to a pan with the oats, cinnamon and milk. Cook over a low heat, stirring occasionally until the oats and grains are soft and the milk absorbed to your preferred consistency (about 10 minutes).

Top with pumpkin seeds, sliced strawberries, blueberries and a little finely chopped mint, if liked.

Granola

Making a batch of your own granola will save money plus you can personalize the mix just the way you like it. This recipe also has less sugar than many shop-bought equivalents.

Makes 1 large jar | Takes 45 minutes

INGREDIENTS

300 g (11 oz) gluten-free
  rolled oats
100 g (3½ oz) pumpkin seeds
100 g (3½ oz) blanched
  whole almonds
150 g (5 oz) whole pecans
100 g (3½ oz) flaked coconut
120 ml (4 fl oz) agave
  syrup or honey
80 ml (3 fl oz) sunflower oil
½ tsp vanilla extract
½ tsp ground cinnamon
a pinch of salt

METHOD

Preheat the oven to 150°C/130°C fan/300°F/gas mark 2 and spray a large, rimmed baking tray (or two smaller ones) lightly with oil or line with baking parchment.

Put the oats in a large mixing bowl with the pumpkin seeds, almonds, pecans and coconut. Now stir together the agave syrup or honey, sunflower oil and vanilla extract in a bowl then pour over your oats mixture. Add the cinnamon plus a pinch of salt and give it all a good stir.

Pour the mix onto the tray and spread out in an even layer before baking for 40–45 minutes or until cooked. Check on it occasionally to make sure it's not burning and stir with a wooden spoon to ensure it toasts evenly. When it's cooked, it'll look golden and toasted all over – remove from the oven and leave to cool before packaging it up in an airtight container.

American-style banana pancakes

These fluffy pancakes are super-easy to make from scratch and are sweetened only with banana and no other added sugar.

Makes 6–8 | Takes 10 minutes

INGREDIENTS

175 g (6 oz) gluten-free
  self-raising flour
1 tsp gluten-free baking powder
1 ripe banana
1 egg
½ tsp vanilla extract
125 ml (4½ fl oz) milk
1 knob of butter for frying
berries, chopped pistachios,
  Greek yoghurt and
  honey to serve

METHOD

Sift the flour and baking powder into a bowl. In a separate bowl, mash the banana with a fork until smooth then whisk in the egg, vanilla and milk. Tip into the flour and whisk to a smooth thick batter (don't worry if there are a few lumps from the banana).

Heat the butter in a frying pan then add about 1½ tbsp of batter per pancake. Cook for 1–2 minutes then flip with a spatula and cook on the other side. Serve with a few berries, chopped pistachios, a dollop of yoghurt and a drizzle of honey.

Breakfast smoothies

This recipe is for a base mix which is either delicious plain or can be varied with the addition of either berries or baby spinach. You can use whatever kind of milk you prefer.

Makes 1 | Takes 5 minutes

INGREDIENTS

250 ml (9 fl oz) milk
1 tbsp gluten-free oats
½ a banana
1 tbsp gluten-free peanut butter
a pinch of cinnamon and either:
a handful of baby spinach
leaves or a handful each of
blueberries and raspberries

METHOD

Blend all the ingredients in a blender until smooth and decant into a glass. You can make this ahead and store in the fridge for a few days.

Traditional pancakes

This batter recipe is easily doubled if you want to make more. For the best result, aim to spread each portion of the mix as thinly as possible in the pan.

Makes 4 | Takes 15 minutes

INGREDIENTS

1 tbsp unsalted butter
70 g (2½ oz) gluten-free
  plain flour
a pinch of salt
100 ml (3½ fl oz) milk
1 egg
lemon juice and sugar, to serve

METHOD

Melt the butter in the pancake pan, leaving a little aside for later. Add the flour to a mixing bowl with a pinch of salt. With a fork, whisk the milk with 50 ml (2 fl oz) water, the melted butter and the egg, then use a balloon whisk to blend the wet ingredients into the flour to make a smooth batter.

Heat the pan over a medium heat and melt the remaining butter. Use a ladle to add batter to the pan, swirling it around until it evenly coats the pan in a thin layer. Cook for about 1 minute then flip and cook until golden. Slide out and serve with lemon juice and sugar.

Houmous jam jar dip

**Houmous takes minutes to make at home. Pack your own crunchy veg dippers
with it and enjoy a nutritious, money-saving snack with no unnecessary
plastic and no stress looking for a gluten-free bite on the move.**

Serves 1 | Takes 10 minutes

INGREDIENTS

1 x 400 g (14 oz) can
  chickpeas, drained

3 tbsp olive oil

1 garlic clove, crushed

1 lemon, juiced

1 tbsp tahini

crudites to serve e.g. carrot,
  pepper and celery sticks,
  mange tout or radishes

METHOD

Add all the houmous ingredients to a food
processor with 3 tbsp of water and a good grinding
each of salt and pepper. Blend until smooth and
check the seasoning, adding more salt or pepper to
taste. Decant into a tall lidded jam jar and top with
the crudites to eat on the go.

Chicken and avocado wrap

This quick-prep wrap travels well and is easily made from shop-bought tortillas and chicken. It's also a good supermarket-sweep option for days when you need something fast and straightforward. Tortillas can be cooked on a griddle from frozen so it's worth building up a freezer stash for meals like this.

Makes 2 | Takes 5 minutes

INGREDIENTS

1 avocado
½ lemon, juiced
1 tbsp olive oil
2 gluten-free wholemeal tortilla wraps
a handful of pine nuts
a handful of cooked chicken, shredded
a handful of basil

METHOD

Blend the avocado, lemon juice and olive oil together in a food processor. Spread each wrap with the mixture, sprinkle with pine nuts and chicken then top with a row of basil leaves and grind over some black pepper. Roll up like a burrito and wrap in paper tied with string.

Rainbow noodle salad

**Rice noodles are your new best friend if you're eating gluten-free.
You can prepare this salad in advance to take to work in a lunchbox.
Watch out for peanuts as they're not always gluten-free.**

Makes 1 | Takes 15 minutes

INGREDIENTS

1 nest of flat rice noodles
a handful of frozen
  edamame beans
a handful of cooked chicken
½ a red pepper, thinly sliced
½ a yellow pepper, thinly sliced
1 small carrot, julienned
a handful of red cabbage,
  very thinly sliced
a handful of mint, finely chopped
a handful of coriander,
  finely chopped
lime, chopped gluten-free
  peanuts and sliced red chilli,
  to garnish

METHOD

Cook the noodles according to pack instructions
and drain well in a sieve. Cook the edamame beans
for a few minutes in simmering water and then
drain as well. Mix together with all the remaining
ingredients and serve topped with lime for
squeezing over, chopped peanuts and a little
sliced red chilli.

Edamame falafel with tabbouleh

Enjoy these delicious falafel warm from the oven for dinner or pack in a lunchbox to eat cold the next day for gluten-free food to go. Nice with a dollop of houmous (p.44).

Serves 2 | Takes 35 minutes

FALAFEL INGREDIENTS

a drizzle of olive oil plus
  extra for baking sheet
½ a red onion, finely chopped
1 garlic clove
75 g (3 oz) frozen edamame beans, thawed
25 g (1 oz) gluten-free bread,
  roughly ripped up
3 dried apricots, roughly chopped
a handful each of coriander and flat-leaf
  parsley, roughly chopped
1 tsp cumin

TABBOULEH INGREDIENTS

50 g (2 oz) quinoa
50 g (2 oz) buckwheat
½ a cucumber, diced
100 g (3½ oz) cherry tomatoes, quartered
1 stick of celery, finely sliced
2 big handfuls of flat-leaf
  parsley, finely chopped
½ a red onion, *very* finely chopped
3 tbsp olive oil
1 lemon, juiced

METHOD

Preheat the oven to 190°C/170°C fan/ 375°F/gas mark 5 and grease a baking sheet. Heat the oil in a pan and sweat the onion and garlic (about 5 minutes). Add the cooked onion to a food processor with the beans, bread, apricots, herbs and cumin. Process until the mixture starts to come away in a ball. Wet your hands and roll the mix into 8 balls. Pop on the baking sheet and cook in the oven for 20 minutes, gently turning halfway through.

Meanwhile put the quinoa and buckwheat in a pan, cover with water and simmer for 15 minutes. Mix together the cucumber, tomatoes, celery, flat-leaf parsley and remaining red onion (*very* finely chopped). Whisk together the olive oil and lemon juice and pour over the vegetables. Drain the grains in a sieve, running under cold water and draining well. Combine with the vegetables and top with the falafel.

Summer rolls

Rice papers and rice noodles are two fantastic staples in a gluten-free kitchen. These summer rolls might look tricky but once you make the first one or two, you'll realize they're actually pretty straightforward. Pack in a lunchbox or make a big batch and serve to a group as finger food.

Makes 12 | Takes 30 minutes

INGREDIENTS

100g (3½ oz) vermicelli
   rice noodles
1 carrot, julienned
a handful of coriander,
   finely chopped
a handful of mint leaves,
   finely chopped
12 large rice paper wrappers
large lettuce leaves
a few handfuls of cooked
   chicken, shredded
lime wedges, for squeezing over
gluten-free sweet chilli
   dipping sauce, for serving

METHOD

Cook the noodles according to pack instructions then drain and set aside. Mix together the carrot and herbs in a bowl and set aside. Fill a dish wide enough to fit your rice paper wrappers with room temperature water.

Immerse a wrapper in the water until it softens then lay it on a clean chopping board. Take a lettuce leaf and fill with a little each of the noodles, carrot, herbs and chicken. Roll up the filled lettuce leaf – this keeps the filling in place and makes the rolls easier to eat. Place the rolled lettuce cup on the wrapper towards the centre left. Fold the top and the bottom of the wrapper inwards, then roll it up lengthways. Slice in half if you like.

Repeat for all 12 rolls and serve with lime wedges for squeezing over plus sweet chilli dipping sauce.

Rainbow veggie bowl

Quinoa and buckwheat are quick-cook gluten-free grains and this recipe is
easily doubled so you can cook it once for dinner and pack some in a lunchbox
for work the next day. It makes a glossy, vibrant and delicious salad.

Serves 2 | Takes 30 minutes

INGREDIENTS

1 red pepper, cut into thin strips

1 orange or yellow pepper,
cut into thin strips

75 g (3 oz) asparagus,
bases removed

1 red onion, cut into
small wedges

35 g (1½ oz) quinoa

35 g (1½ oz) buckwheat

1 small red chilli

a handful of either (or a
mix of) basil, coriander,
mint or flat-leaf parsley

1 lemon, juiced and zested

1 tbsp olive oil

½ tbsp red wine vinegar

METHOD

Heat a griddle pan then cook the veg, charring
on all sides. Add the griddled veg to a mixing
bowl. At the same time, boil the quinoa and the
buckwheat together in salted water until tender
(10–15 minutes).

Meanwhile, top and tail then deseed your chilli,
slice into slivers and finely chop. Now finely chop
your herbs. Zest and juice your lemon. Whisk the
lemon juice with the olive oil and red wine vinegar
then season with salt and pepper.

Drain the grains and mix with the griddled veg,
chilli, herbs and lemon zest. Pour over the dressing,
taste and add a little more salt and pepper if you
like. Can be served hot or cold.

Caesar salad

Crunchy roasted chickpeas make nutritious gluten-free croutons in this lighter version of Caesar salad. If you're in a rush, you can substitute the chickpeas for croutons by toasting some gluten-free bread and cutting it into small cubes.

Serves 2 | Takes 45 minutes

INGREDIENTS

1 x 400 g (14 oz) can chickpeas, drained
1 tbsp olive oil
1 garlic clove
½ tsp dried oregano
3 tbsp Greek yoghurt
2 anchovy fillets, drained
½ a lemon, juiced
20 g (¾ oz) parmesan
1 Little Gem lettuce
a little watercress and baby-leaf spinach
cooked chicken breast, shredded

METHOD

Preheat the oven to 180°C/160°C fan/350°F/gas mark 4. Toss the drained chickpeas in a bowl with the oil, garlic and oregano, season with salt and pepper and spread out on baking tray lined with baking paper. Pop in the oven for 40 minutes to crisp up like croutons, shaking the tray lightly halfway through to roll the chickpeas.

Meanwhile, put the yoghurt, anchovies, lemon juice and half the parmesan in a blender. Whizz until smooth then season. Arrange the lettuce, watercress, spinach and chicken in bowls. Top with the crunchy chickpeas, the dressing and the remaining cheese, grated over. If you are packing this in a lunchbox, keep the dressing in a separate little pot and mix in before serving.

Chocolate brownie bites

Dates, not refined sugar, provide all the sweetness in these salted hazelnut chocolate energy bites. Get into the habit of prepping a jar once a week and you'll always have a supply of portable sweet treats.

Makes 20 | Takes 10 minutes

INGREDIENTS

20 medjool dates, pitted
50 g (2 oz) gluten-free oats
2 tsp vanilla essence
4 tbsp cocoa powder
a pinch of salt
2 tbsp toasted chopped
  hazelnuts

METHOD

Add all the ingredients except for the hazelnuts to a food processor and blend until well combined and the mixture comes away in a ball (this will take a few minutes). Spread the hazelnuts out on a plate. With wet hands roll the mixture into 20 little balls then roll each in the hazelnuts to coat. Store for up to a week in a jar or tin.

Chocolate gingernut bark

It takes just minutes to prep your own grown-up, ginger-spiked little chocolate bars, which will sit quite happily in the fridge waiting to be called upon for your next coffee break or sweet craving.

Makes 1 slab | Takes 10 minutes plus setting

INGREDIENTS

300 g (11 oz) gluten-free dark or milk chocolate

50 g (2 oz) pistachio nuts

30 g (1 oz) crystallized stem ginger

METHOD

Line a baking sheet with greaseproof paper. Break up your bars of chocolate. The easiest way to do this is to smash them on a chopping board or between your fingers while they're still in the foil wrapper. Melt the chocolate gently in a bain-marie (a heatproof bowl set over a pan of simmering water).

Roughly chop the pistachio nuts and ginger on a chopping board. Once the chocolate is melted take it off the heat and stir in most of the nuts and ginger. Pour onto the prepped tray, sprinkle over the remaining nuts and ginger and pop in the fridge to set. It doesn't matter whether or not it fills the tray, as long as it's relatively even. Once set, chop it up into chunks or wedges with a sharp knife and store in a tin in the fridge.

DINNER

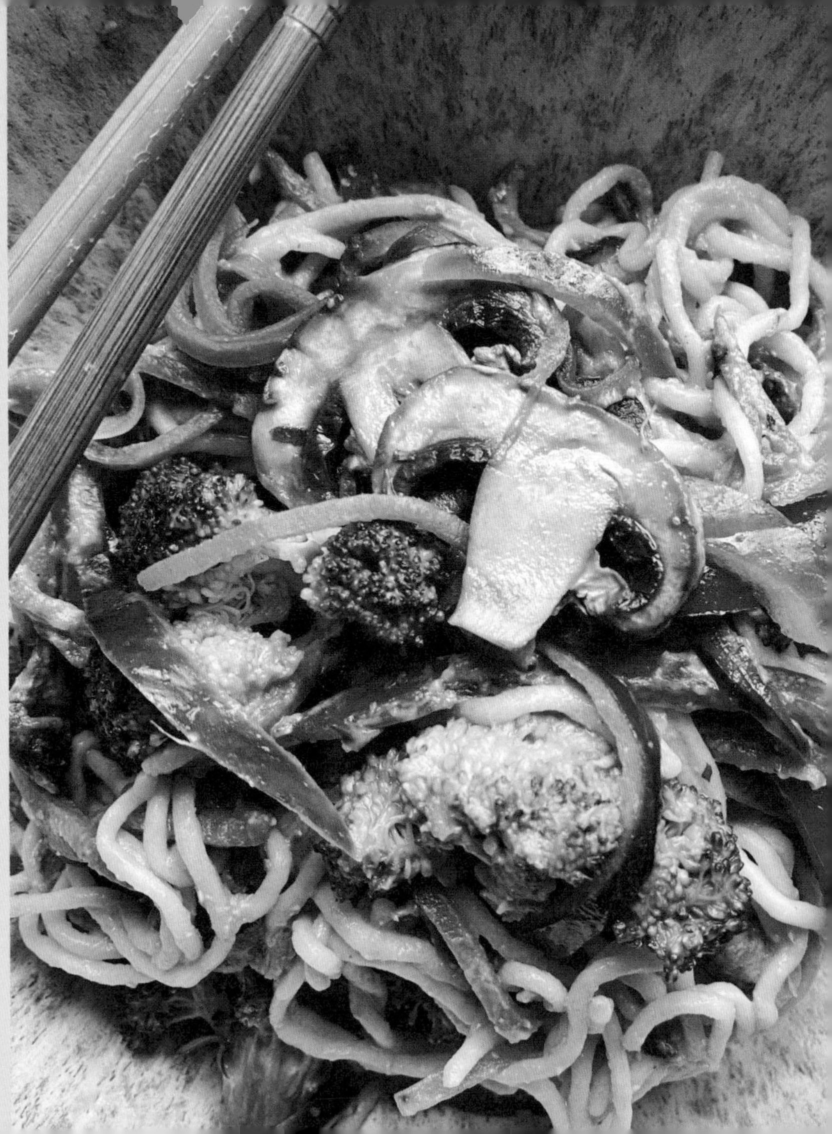

Chicken and rice soup

A comforting little bowl of soup that's very quick and easy to pull together and uses up veg that is often hanging around in the fridge. You can make this ahead and store in the fridge or freezer to reheat for another day.

Serves 2 | Takes 20 minutes

INGREDIENTS

1 tbsp olive oil
1 onion, finely chopped
1 carrot, diced
1 stick of celery, diced
a few sprigs of thyme, leaves picked
600 ml (1 pint) gluten-free chicken or vegetable stock
2 chicken breasts, cut into small pieces
a pouch of cooked brown basmati rice
a handful of frozen peas

METHOD

Sweat the onion, carrot and celery in the oil for 5 minutes. Add half of the thyme along with the stock.

Add the chicken to the pan and bring the soup up to a gentle simmer. Put the lid on and poach the chicken until cooked through (about 10 minutes).

Add the cooked brown rice and peas for the last few minutes of cooking along with the remaining thyme. Ladle into bowls to serve.

Green macaroni cheese

Frozen peas and spinach form the basis of the sauce in this green veggie mac and cheese. It's simple to make using gluten-free pasta and breadcrumbs and means no missing out when you want a dose of comfort food.

Serves 2–4 | Takes 35 minutes

INGREDIENTS

600 ml (1 pint) whole milk
5 discs of frozen spinach
2 handfuls of frozen peas
1 tbsp butter
1 tbsp gluten-free plain flour
1 tsp gluten-free mustard powder
2 handfuls of grated cheddar
500 g (18 oz) gluten-free
  macaroni
125 g (4½ oz) gluten-free bread
1 garlic clove
1 tbsp olive oil

METHOD

Heat the milk and frozen vegetables together over a gentle heat until the spinach is thawed (about 5 minutes). Blend in a food processor. Melt the butter in a non-stick pan, stir in the flour and mustard powder then whisk in the green milk a bit at a time to give a nice glossy sauce. Season with salt and pepper and stir in the cheese.

Preheat the oven to 200°C/180°C fan/400°F/ gas mark 6. Cook the macaroni according to pack instructions then drain. While the pasta is cooking, blend the bread into breadcrumbs with the whole clove of garlic and olive oil in the food processor or blender (no need to clean from the sauce). Ensure the garlic is finely chopped in the blender.

Stir the sauce into the pasta in an oven dish, top with the garlicky breadcrumbs and cook for 15 minutes until golden, crisp and bubbly.

Halloumi burger

You're only ever a brief supermarket sweep away from assembling this nutritious standby. Just buy pesto, veggies and a pack of halloumi and make in minutes. Get into the habit of keeping sliced ciabatta or burger buns in your freezer as you can quickly defrost these in your toaster.

Makes 2 | Takes 15 minutes

INGREDIENTS

1 small courgette, sliced
1 yellow pepper, cut
  into thick strips
1 pack of halloumi cheese, sliced
2 gluten-free ciabatta
  rolls or burger buns
2 tbsp fresh pesto
4 Little Gem lettuce
  leaves, thinly sliced
1 beef tomato, sliced

METHOD

Heat a griddle pan over a high heat and cook the courgette and pepper until charred on all sides. Remove to a plate and cook the halloumi cheese on the griddle until charred on both sides.

Meanwhile split the buns and lightly toast. Once toasted, spread the bases with pesto, then add lettuce leaves and a few slices of tomato. Top with yellow pepper, halloumi and then courgette, then pop the other bun half on the top and serve.

Japanese noodles

Sometimes called konjac noodles, shirataki noodles come wok-ready in the pack and are like gluten-free egg noodles. This recipe is a bowl of gingery, garlicky, slurpy noodles, just like those served in your favourite Japanese restaurant.

Serves 2 | Takes 20 minutes

INGREDIENTS

1 tsp sesame oil, plus a drizzle more for the pan

2 tbsp white miso paste

2 tsp gluten-free soy sauce or tamari

1 garlic clove, crushed

a thumb-sized piece of ginger, peeled and grated

1 red onion, thinly sliced

1 red pepper, thinly sliced

3 chestnut mushrooms, sliced

1 small crown of broccoli, cut into very small florets

1 carrot, peeled and julienned

1 pack of shirataki (or konjac) noodles

METHOD

Make the miso sauce by mixing 1 tsp sesame oil with the miso, soy sauce or tamari, crushed garlic and grated ginger. Stir together with 2 tbsp of water.

Heat a drizzle more oil in a wok or large frying pan over a high heat. Add the onion, pepper, mushrooms and broccoli and stir fry for 10 minutes, tossing regularly. Add the julienned carrot, noodles and miso sauce and stir-fry for another 2 minutes until everything is piping hot and coated in the sauce. Divide between bowls and serve.

Cheat's chicken tikka

Sometimes a couple of shop-bought short cuts can be invaluable to help you make a fresh plate of food. Stock your cupboard with pouches of pilau rice and tikka marinade for a taste of your favourite takeaway with next-to-no effort. You will need wooden or metal skewers for this recipe.

Serves 2 | Takes 35 minutes + 30 minutes marinading

INGREDIENTS

1 shop-bought gluten-free tikka marinade
1 tbsp natural yoghurt
2 chicken breast fillets, cut into strips
2 pouches of gluten-free pilau rice
a handful of coriander, chopped
1 tsp nigella seeds
lime wedges, to squeeze over

METHOD

Add the marinade and yoghurt to the chicken strips in a bowl and stir. Cover in cling film, or pop in a lidded Tupperware, and chill in the fridge for at least 30 minutes (or earlier in the day and return to it when you're ready to make dinner).

Brush an oven-friendly griddle pan with a little oil. Preheat the oven to 220°C/200°C fan/425°F/gas mark 7, popping the griddle pan into the oven to heat up at the same time. Meanwhile, thread the chicken strips onto the skewers. Remove the hot griddle pan from the oven and lay the skewers gently onto the pan. Return to the oven and cook for 25 minutes, turning halfway through, until the chicken is charred and thoroughly cooked.

Towards the end of cooking, heat the pilau rice. Serve the chicken skewers on the rice, sprinkled with coriander and nigella seeds, plus lime wedges to squeeze over.

Sushi poke bowls

A lot of shop-bought sushi contains gluten either from soy, panko breadcrumbs or tempura, or from cross-contamination. These poke bowls are a taste of sushi for coeliacs and can be pulled together very easily via a quick trip to the supermarket.

Serves 2 | Takes 10 minutes

INGREDIENTS

a pouch of cooked jasmine rice

1 tsp sushi vinegar

2 handfuls of frozen
  edamame beans

1 avocado, diced

½ a cucumber, diced

1 small carrot, peeled
  and julienned

100 g (3½ oz) smoked salmon

black and white sesame
  seeds, to serve

gluten-free soy sauce, to serve

METHOD

Heat the rice in a pan for 5 minutes then take off the heat and stir through the sushi vinegar. At the same time, heat the edamame beans for a few minutes in boiling water then drain.

Meanwhile, prep all your veg. Assemble the bowls by tearing the salmon into strips and adding alongside everything else. Sprinkle with the sesame seeds and serve with gluten-free soy.

Pinwheel salads

You can batch cook double quantities of the roasted veg in this salad to use in lunchboxes and dinners across the week. If you don't have time to cook any veg, you can make a raw veg pinwheel salad instead in a matter of minutes using chopped peppers, cherry tomatoes, cucumber, flat-leaf parsley, shop-bought cooked chicken and a can or pouch of lentils. Then just dress with olive oil, salt and pepper.

Serves 2 | Takes 35 minutes

INGREDIENTS

2 red onions, cut into wedges
1 red pepper, diced
1 yellow pepper, diced
1 small courgette, diced
1 small aubergine, cut into
   2 cm (¾ in.) cubes
2 garlic cloves
2 tsp dried oregano
3 tbsp olive oil
150 g (5 oz) gluten-free maize
   couscous (or use rice)
a handful of basil, to serve

METHOD

Preheat the oven to 220°C/200°C fan/425°F/ gas mark 7. Put the onions, peppers, courgette and aubergine into a roasting dish and spread out evenly. Crush over the garlic, scatter with the oregano and drizzle over the olive oil. Ensure everything is well coated and season with salt and pepper. Roast for 20 minutes then carefully turn and roast for a further 10 minutes.

Cover the couscous (just) with boiling water in a bowl and leave to soften. After about 5 minutes it will have absorbed the liquid. Fluff with a fork and season with salt and pepper. Serve the roasted veg with the maize couscous (or rice) and rip up the basil over the top, plus a little extra olive oil drizzled over.

Fishfinger sandwich

Supermarkets do sometimes stock gluten-free fishfingers but if the craving strikes and you can't find them, this is how to make your own. They're very easy and taste fantastic homemade – once you've tried them this way, you might never go back.

Serves 2 | Takes 20 minutes

INGREDIENTS

cod fillet (approx. 250 g/9 oz)
3 tbsp cornflour
1 egg, beaten
4 tbsp gluten-free breadcrumbs
  (brioche works best)
sliced gluten-free bread
Little Gem lettuce
  leaves, to serve
tartare sauce and lemon
  wedges, to serve

METHOD

Preheat the oven to 220°C/200°C fan/425°F/ gas mark 7 and oil a baking sheet with a good coating of oil.

Cut your fish into strips using a sharp knife. Get three shallow bowls. Add the cornflour to one, the beaten egg to another and the breadcrumbs to the third. Season the cornflour well with salt and pepper. Keeping one hand flour-free, dip each fishfinger first into the cornflour to coat all over, tapping off any excess, then into the egg and then into the breadcrumbs. Place each on the baking sheet turning gently in the oil to coat on both sides.

Bake for 20 minutes until golden. Squeeze with a little lemon juice and make a sandwich with Little Gem lettuce and tartare sauce.

Extra green pesto pasta

Adding spiralized courgette to pesto pasta adds extra colour as well as nutrients. If you don't have a spiralizer, you can just grate it in.

Serves 2 | Takes 15 minutes

INGREDIENTS

1 garlic clove, peeled
5 tbsp extra virgin olive oil
50 g (2 oz) basil
50 g (2 oz) pine nuts
25 g (1 oz) parmesan,
  plus extra to serve
200 g (7 oz) gluten-free
  spaghetti
1 small courgette, spiralized

METHOD

Pop the peeled garlic clove into a food processor with the olive oil and basil and blitz. Add the pine nuts and pulse to keep the nuts a little chunkier. Grate the parmesan and stir into the pesto. Season with salt and pepper.

Meanwhile cook the spaghetti according to pack instructions, adding the spiralized courgette for the last minute of cooking to just soften. Drain and mix with the pesto. Serve scattered with extra grated parmesan.

Veggie fried rice

A super-quick standby for busy nights, this delicious garlic, lime and ginger-spiked fried rice uses up bits and pieces of veg from your fridge alongside pouches of precooked rice to make a warming, nourishing bowl of food. Store fresh ginger in your freezer (it grates straight from frozen).

Serves 2 | Takes 15 minutes

INGREDIENTS

1 carrot, peeled and grated

a handful of spring greens or Savoy cabbage, finely shredded

1 onion, finely sliced

a glug of sesame oil

a thumb-sized piece of fresh ginger, grated

1 garlic clove, crushed

2 pouches of precooked rice

1 small bunch of coriander, chopped

a drizzle of gluten-free soy sauce or tamari

lime wedges, to serve

METHOD

Add the carrot, spring greens (or Savoy cabbage) and onion to a wok or large frying pan with a glug of sesame oil, the grated ginger and the crushed garlic.

Stir-fry the vegetables until a little softened and charred, then add the rice pouches and warm through until piping hot and beginning to crisp and catch in places. Serve with chopped coriander and a little soy sauce or tamari and lime wedges to squeeze over.

Quick and easy pizza

This pizza dough is simple to make from scratch, is crispy and chars nicely.

Makes 2 | Takes 45 minutes

INGREDIENTS

12 standard sized
  tomatoes, halved
1 garlic clove, crushed
1 tsp dried oregano
a drizzle of olive
  oil, plus extra
  for the bases
300 g (11 oz)
  gluten-free
  self-raising flour
2 tsp baking powder
1 tsp salt
300 g (11 oz)
  natural yoghurt
grated mozzarella or
  cheddar or a mix
a sprinkle of polenta
  for baking
a few basil leaves

METHOD

Preheat the oven to 240°C/220°C fan/475°F/gas mark 9 and add the tomatoes to a roasting tin with the garlic, oregano and plenty of salt and pepper. Drizzle with olive oil and give everything a shake. Roast for 20 minutes until just charred, then blend and place two pizza trays in the oven to heat up.

Meanwhile, make your dough. Combine flour, baking powder and salt in a bowl then pour in the yoghurt. Begin to bring together with a fork then knead together into a ball in the bowl. Divide into two equal pieces and roll each into a smooth ball between your palms. Place each on a sheet of baking parchment which you have first lightly sprinkled with polenta (this makes the bases crispy). Put a second sheet of parchment on top of each dough ball and roll into discs using a rolling pin over the top sheet. Remove the top sheet and spread with tomato sauce leaving a border around the circumference and scatter over the cheese. Brush the pizza borders with a little olive oil. Get the hot trays out of the oven and transfer the pizzas, still on the bottom sheet of parchment, straight to the trays.

Bake for 12 minutes or until charred at the edges. Slide off the parchment onto plates and top with lots of basil to serve.

Cheat's kedgeree

A pack of smoked salmon reduces cooking time in this cheat's kedgeree. You can also keep packs of frozen smoked salmon trimmings in the freezer and cook from frozen in the recipe — just add alongside the frozen peas and ensure it's all piping hot for a delicious dinner pulled together from your freezer.

Serves 2 | Takes 25 minutes

INGREDIENTS

a drizzle of olive oil
½ an onion, finely chopped
1 garlic clove, crushed
1 tsp curry powder
220 g (8 oz) basmati rice
1 free-range egg
a handful of frozen peas
100 g (3½ oz) smoked salmon
a handful of coriander,
  finely chopped
a wedge of lemon, to serve

METHOD

Heat the oil in a frying pan and soften the onion with the garlic and curry powder stirred through it.

Meanwhile, cook the rice for 10 minutes in plenty of water and pop the egg into the same pan. Drain the rice and set the egg aside until cool enough to handle.

Add the drained rice to the onion with the frozen peas. Tear up the smoked salmon into little pieces and stir it all together over the heat for a few minutes. The fish and peas will cook quickly in the hot pan.

Peel the egg and slice into quarters. Ensure the fish, peas and rice are piping hot and cooked through then stir in the chopped coriander and top with the egg. Serve with lemon for squeezing over and season with black pepper.

Nachos

This is a lighter version of everyone's favourite movie night meal, with plenty of fresh guacamole, tomatoes, sweetcorn and peppers. Most corn chips are gluten-free but always double-check the label.

Serves 2 | Takes 15 minutes

INGREDIENTS

1 bag gluten-free nacho chips

a small can of sweetcorn (no-added sugar or salt), drained

1 red pepper, diced

2 handfuls of cooked shredded chicken

3 handfuls of grated cheddar

1 large avocado, mashed

2 handfuls of cherry tomatoes, finely chopped

a small bunch of coriander, finely chopped

1 lime

METHOD

Preheat the oven to 220°C/200°C fan/425°F/gas mark 7. Divide the nacho chips between two baking trays or small oven dishes. Top with the sweetcorn, diced pepper, cooked shredded chicken and then the grated cheese. Cook until the cheese is melted and golden, and the chips are starting to brown at the edges.

Top with spoonfuls of the mashed avocado and chopped tomatoes, scatter over plenty of chopped coriander and serve with lime to squeeze over.

Lentil polpette

Ground almonds take the place of breadcrumbs in these meatless meatballs. Cooked lentils are a good standby to have in your cupboard alongside canned tomatoes and packs of spaghetti.

Serves 2 | Takes 30 minutes

INGREDIENTS

1 x 400 g (14 oz) can Puy or green lentils
4 tbsp olive oil
1 onion, finely chopped
2 garlic cloves
½ tsp paprika
a handful of flat-leaf parsley, finely chopped
2 tbsp ground almonds
1 x 400 g (14 oz) can chopped tomatoes
a pinch of chilli flakes
200 g (7 oz) gluten-free spaghetti
a handful of basil leaves, to garnish

METHOD

Drain the lentils really well by rubbing the moisture out of them through a sieve with the back of a spoon. Heat 2 tbsp of the oil in a large frying pan or shallow casserole dish over a medium heat. Add the onion and soften for 5 minutes then crush in the garlic and cook for a few minutes more. Tip half of this onion mix into a food processor along with the drained lentils, paprika, parsley and ground almonds. Pulse to a coarse mixture.

Put the canned tomatoes and chilli flakes in the pan with the rest of the onion and simmer for about 10 minutes. Cook the spaghetti.

Meanwhile, heat the remaining 2 tbsp of the oil in a frying pan over a medium heat. With wet hands, roll the lentil mixture into 8 balls, flatten slightly and fry for about 10 minutes, or until firm enough to flip with a spoon, then gently turn and brown for a few more minutes on the other side until golden all over. Drain the spaghetti, spoon over the hot tomato sauce, top with the polpette and tear over a little basil to serve.

Cheat's paella

This quick paella is made with frozen prawns and jarred griddled peppers
meaning you can pull together a fantastic dinner with little forethought.
Made all in one pan with minimal fuss and lots of punchy flavours.

Serves 2 | Takes 35 minutes

INGREDIENTS

2 tbsp olive oil

1 red onion, diced

1 garlic clove

½ tsp paprika

½ tsp turmeric

a pinch of chilli flakes

100 g (3½ oz) risotto rice

500 ml (18 fl oz) gluten-free
  vegetable stock

1 bag frozen tiger prawns

2 roasted red peppers from
  a jar, chopped into strips

a handful of cherry tomatoes,
  roughly chopped

a handful of flat-leaf
  parsley, finely chopped

1 lemon, cut into wedges

METHOD

Heat the oil in a large, lidded frying pan or casserole
dish then add the onion and crush in the garlic.
Soften for 5 minutes then season with salt and
pepper and add the paprika, turmeric and chilli
flakes. Cook for a few more minutes then stir in the
rice and stock. Pop the lid on and cook for about
20 minutes over a low heat until the stock is
absorbed. Stir on and off.

Towards the end of cooking, stir through the frozen
prawns, peppers and tomatoes. Taste the rice
to ensure it's cooked and make sure the prawns,
peppers and tomatoes are all piping hot and
cooked through. Stir in the flat-leaf parsley and
serve with lemon wedges on the side to squeeze
over, and plenty of black pepper.

Smoked salmon hotcakes

These delicious triple-corn hotcakes are made from polenta, cornflour and sweetcorn. The batter is foolproof; nice and thick and very easy to flip in the pan. You don't even need to get your weighing scales out to make this easy recipe.

Serves 2 | Takes 15 minutes

INGREDIENTS

2 tbsp polenta
2 tbsp cornflour
2 eggs
2 spring onions, chopped
a small can of sweetcorn
  (no-added sugar or
  salt), drained
a drizzle of olive oil
smoked salmon, to serve
2 tbsp Greek yoghurt, to serve
a handful of dill, chopped
lemon wedges, to squeeze over

METHOD

Mix together the polenta and cornflour in a bowl. Beat the eggs, then stir into the polenta and cornflour with the spring onions and sweetcorn. Season with a little salt and pepper.

Heat the oil in a large frying pan then drop spoonfuls of the batter into the pan. The mixture makes four hotcakes so, depending on the size of your pan, you'll be able to do them all at once or in two batches. Flip them over after a few minutes and cook on the other side. Serve with smoked salmon, a dollop of yoghurt mixed with a little chopped dill, plus lemon wedges to squeeze over.

Sweet potato soup

There's very little prep required in making this wholesome and cheerful, brightly coloured soup. Ginger and orange add plenty of flavour and toasted gluten-free bread makes quick cheat's croutons.

Serves 2 | Takes 40 minutes

INGREDIENTS

2 sweet potatoes

1 onion

a drizzle of olive oil

1 orange

1 thumb-sized piece of fresh ginger, grated

2 slices of gluten-free granary bread

a dollop of Greek yoghurt, to serve

METHOD

Peel and then dice the sweet potatoes and the onion then put in a pan with a glug of olive oil, plus the zest and juice of one orange and the grated ginger.

Cook over a medium heat for 15 minutes, stirring on and off to soften a little, and then add 750 ml (26 fl oz) boiled water from the kettle to the pan. Bring back to the boil and then simmer for 20 minutes.

Toast the bread and cut into small square croutons. Blend the soup until smooth – you can add a splash of water to loosen if needed and also leave it a little chunky or make it completely smooth, depending on what you fancy. Serve with a swirl of Greek yoghurt, the toasted croutons and lots of black pepper ground over.

Salmon with greens and grains

Precooked pouches of grains and rice are a very useful standby in your gluten-free kitchen. Pick up some salmon, lemon and herbs and make a nourishing meal in minutes with staples like frozen peas, garlic and mustard. If you can't find a pouch of grains and rice, just use a pouch of plain rice.

Serves 2 | Takes 20 minutes

INGREDIENTS

2 portions of salmon fillet

2 tbsp olive oil, plus a drizzle extra for cooking

½ tsp honey

½ tsp wholegrain mustard

1 lemon, juiced

1 garlic clove

a few baby spinach leaves

250 g (9 oz) pouch of gluten-free wholegrain rice and quinoa

a handful of frozen peas

a handful of flat-leaf parsley, finely chopped

METHOD

Preheat the oven to 180°C/160°C fan/350°F/ gas mark 4 and cook the salmon in a lightly oiled dish for 20 minutes.

Meanwhile, mix 2 tbsp oil with the honey, mustard, lemon juice, salt and pepper. Heat a drizzle more oil in a pan, crush in the garlic and cook until soft. Stack the spinach leaves one on top of each other, roll up together then thinly slice. Add to the pan with the rice, grains and peas and heat it all through together.

Mix in the dressing, top with the cooked salmon and scatter over the parsley to serve.

Pasta puttanesca

This delicious, quick and easy midweek meal is made from predominantly cupboard staples. Get into the habit of keeping capers, olives and anchovies to hand and all you need grab on the way home are tomatoes and basil.

Serves 2 | Takes 10 minutes

INGREDIENTS

200 g (7 oz) gluten-free spaghetti

a drizzle of olive oil

1 garlic clove, crushed

a pinch of dried chilli flakes

300 g (11 oz) baby plum or cherry tomatoes, diced

1 tbsp capers

a handful of pitted black olives, sliced in half

1 small can of anchovies, drained and finely chopped

a handful of basil, to serve

METHOD

Cook the spaghetti according to pack instructions. Meanwhile, drizzle a pan with olive oil and add the crushed garlic, chilli flakes, diced tomatoes, capers, olives and anchovies. Cook gently for about 5 minutes. Drain the pasta and combine with the sauce, scattering with basil to serve.

Arancini

Make sure your leftover risotto rice is well chilled and not too wet before making these arancini. The risotto recipe on p.104 makes enough for dinner for two with half as much again left over – enough to make this arancini recipe for lunch the next day.

Makes 8 arancini | Takes 30 minutes

INGREDIENTS

Tomato risotto, chilled
(see above)

25 g (1 oz) mozzarella,
finely chopped

1 pot of fresh shop-bought pesto
(or make your own, see p.80)

50 g (2 oz) gluten-free
plain flour

1 egg, beaten

70 g (2½ oz) gluten-free
breadcrumbs (brioche is best)

green salad, to serve

METHOD

Preheat the oven to 220°C/200°C fan/425°F/gas mark 7 and oil a baking sheet well. With wet hands, take a little risotto and roll into a ball, then flatten. Add a little mozzarella to the middle plus a tsp of pesto. Fold the rice around the filling in the middle and re-roll the arancini into a ball. Repeat until all the mixture is used up.

Keeping one hand clean, roll each ball into first flour to coat lightly all over, then egg and then breadcrumbs. Repeat with all the arancini, popping on the baking sheet as you go.

Gently turn the arancini in the oil on the baking sheet then cook for 10–15 minutes until golden all over. Serve with a green salad.

Cheat's tomato risotto

A mix of cherry and standard tomatoes is nice in this risotto, but any kind is delicious. This method avoids the need to keep stirring the rice all the time – good for busy nights. The recipe makes enough for dinner for two with the same quantity again left over to turn into Arancini the next day (see p.103). You can also just chill the remainder in the fridge and reheat the next day as it is.

Serves 2 with leftovers for Arancini | Takes 30 minutes

INGREDIENTS

a drizzle of olive oil

1 onion, finely diced

1 garlic clove, crushed

1 l (35 fl oz) gluten-free chicken or vegetable stock

a good pinch of saffron threads

350 g (12 oz) arborio rice

450 g (16 oz) tomatoes, finely chopped

65 g (2½ oz) parmesan, grated

a knob of butter

a good handful of flat-leaf parsley, finely chopped

METHOD

Heat the olive oil in a large pan then add the onion and garlic, cooking until soft. Add the stock, saffron, rice and tomatoes to the pan and bring to the boil. Turn down the heat and simmer gently until the rice is cooked and the stock is absorbed (20–25 minutes). Stir on and off with a wooden spoon, breaking down the tomatoes with the back of a spoon. Stir in the parmesan and a knob of butter and season with plenty of black pepper. Stir in the finely chopped flat-leaf parsley to serve.

Storecupboard smoky bean stew

This nourishing bowl is made from cupboard beans and tomatoes. Look out for jarred cannellini beans which are extra flavoursome and hold their shape well.

Serves 2 | Takes 25 minutes

INGREDIENTS

1 tbsp olive oil, plus
   extra to serve
1 onion, finely chopped
1 garlic clove, crushed
1 tsp paprika
1 x 400 g (14 oz) can
   chopped tomatoes
200 ml (7 fl oz) gluten-free
   vegetable stock
700 g (25 oz) jar cooked
   cannellini beans
2 tbsp crème fraîche
a handful of rocket leaves and/
   or chopped flat-leaf parsley

METHOD

Heat the oil in a large saucepan over a medium heat and sweat the onion for 5 minutes. Add the garlic and paprika and cook for a minute more, then tip in the tomatoes and stock. Simmer for 15 minutes until thickened then add the cannellini beans from the jar (don't drain as the jarred stock is full of flavour) and cook through for 3–5 minutes until piping hot and the sauce is reduced. Serve in bowls topped with a dollop of crème fraîche to stir through, a handful of rocket leaves and/or chopped flat-leaf parsley and plenty of black pepper.

Pasta veggienese

This freezable veggie ragu recipe is easily doubled so you can batch cook, portion it up and keep it on hand for days when you have less time to cook from scratch. Experiment with dried pasta shapes to find your favourites — you'll find most shop-bought brands match the quality of standard pasta.

Serves 4 | Takes 45 minutes

INGREDIENTS

1 tbsp olive oil

1 onion, diced

1 carrot, diced

2 sticks of celery, diced

1 garlic clove, crushed

250 g (9 oz) dried red lentils

1 x 400 g (14 oz) can chopped tomatoes

1 tsp dried oregano

500 ml (18 fl oz) gluten-free vegetable stock

500 g (18 oz) gluten-free pasta

a handful of flat-leaf parsley, chopped

grated parmesan, to serve

dressed green salad, to serve

METHOD

Heat the oil in a large pan and add the onions, carrots, celery and garlic. Soften gently for 15 minutes. Stir in the lentils, chopped tomatoes, oregano and stock. Bring to a simmer, cover with a lid then cook over a low heat for 30 minutes until the lentils are tender and saucy. Season.

Meanwhile cook the pasta following pack instructions then drain and mix with the sauce. Scatter over the parsley and parmesan and serve with a green salad on the side.

BAKING

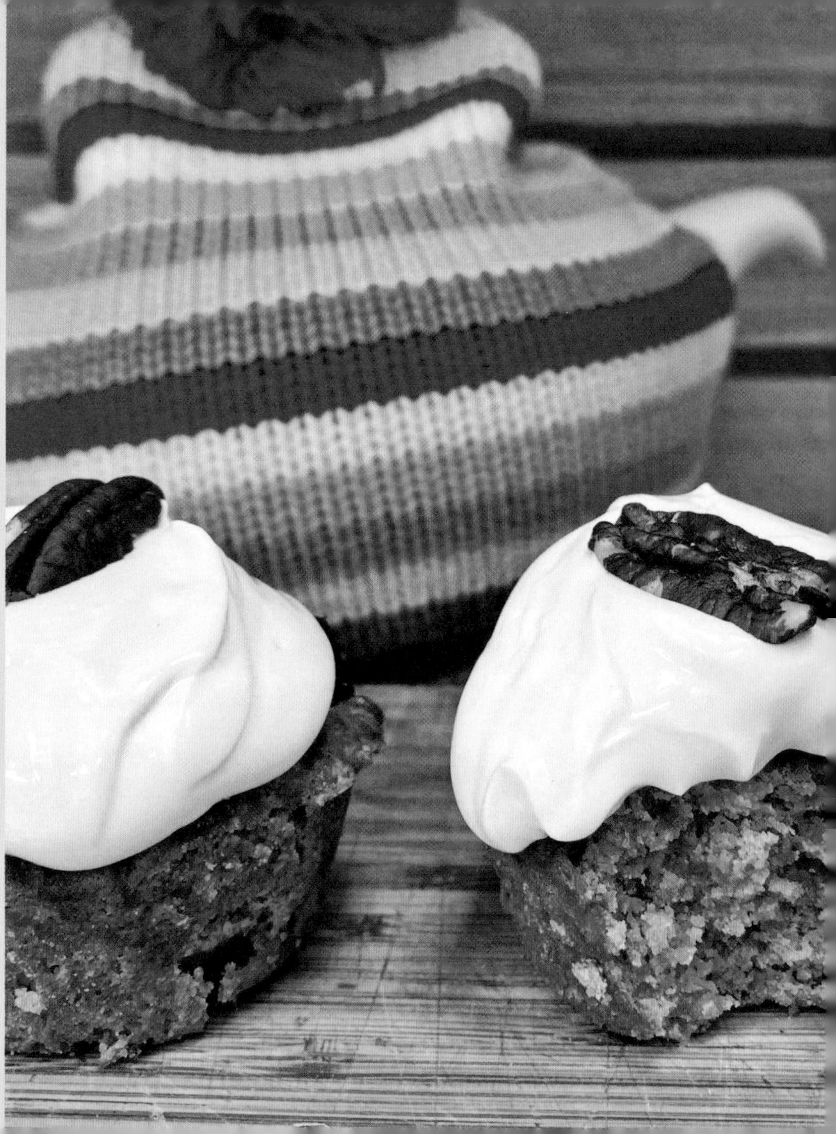

Easy white loaf

A foolproof and fuss-free crusty and fluffy loaf is top of every gluten-free baker's list. This one is delicious for sandwiches, dipping in soups and can also be frozen sliced, and popped in the toaster for breakfast. Check that the bread flour you are using has xanthan gum included in the blend.

Makes 1 loaf | Takes 1 hour

INGREDIENTS

400 ml (14 fl oz) warm water
1 tbsp caster sugar
2 tsp gluten-free quick yeast
500 g (18 oz) gluten-free white bread flour
4 tsp baking powder
½ tsp salt
1½ tsp cider vinegar
4 tbsp olive oil
1 egg

METHOD

Grease a 1 lb (450 g) loaf tin. Whisk together the warm water, caster sugar and yeast in a bowl and set aside for 10 minutes until frothy. Meanwhile, sift the flour, baking powder and salt in a large mixing bowl. Once the water and yeast mix is frothy, add the cider vinegar, olive oil and egg and whisk again to combine.

Pour the mixture into the flour and fold together with a spatula until fully combined. The dough will look a bit like a thick, spongey cake batter. Use a spatula to transfer the dough to your prepared bread tin, smoothing the top with the spatula. Set aside for 15 minutes somewhere warm and preheat the oven to 200°C/180°C fan/400°F/gas mark 6. Bake in the centre of the oven for 50 minutes until golden brown. Remove your bread from the tin and leave to cool on a wire rack. Don't be tempted to try to slice it until it is cool or it may crumble.

Seeded oat bread

This fluffy soda bread is very easy and looks fantastic with its crispy seeded crust. Excellent toasted or just spread with butter. Make sure your bicarbonate is fresh and don't delay getting it in the oven once mixed; together these tips will give you the best rise on your loaf.

Makes 1 loaf | Takes 1 hour 10 minutes

INGREDIENTS

120 g (4½ oz) gluten-free oats

230 g (8 oz) gluten-free plain flour

1 tbsp caster sugar

75 g (3 oz) mixed seeds (sunflower, pumpkin, sesame and poppy)

½ tsp salt

2 tsp bicarbonate of soda

2 tbsp sunflower oil, plus extra for the tin

500 g (18 oz) natural yoghurt

METHOD

Preheat the oven to 180°C/160°C fan/350°F/gas mark 4 and grease and line a 1 lb (450 g) loaf tin with baking parchment. Add the oats, flour, sugar and most of the seeds to a large mixing bowl then sprinkle over the salt and bicarbonate of soda. Mix together the oil and yoghurt until fully combined then tip into the oat mixture.

Stir everything together until thoroughly combined then spoon into the prepared tin. Flatten the top slightly with the back of a spoon then scatter over the remaining seeds, pressing down gently with the spoon so that they stick to the dough.

Bake for 1 hour then carefully turn out onto a wire rack to cool completely before slicing. You can freeze this sliced and eat it toasted for breakfast with nut butter, blueberries and banana (see p.30).

Cornbread

Cornbread should be served toasted or griddled, then buttered. You can also try topping toasted slices with either smashed avocado or spicy tomato relish, or serve toast soldiers with a bowl of chilli or bean stew (see p.107), as is traditional in the US.

Makes 1 loaf | Takes 50 minutes

INGREDIENTS

75 g (3 oz) unsalted butter
1 x 284 ml (10 fl oz)
  pot of buttermilk
135 ml (5 fl oz) milk
1 egg, beaten
170 g (6 oz) polenta
120 g (4½ oz) cheddar, grated
250 g (9 oz) gluten-free
  plain flour
2½ tsp gluten-free baking powder
1 tsp salt

METHOD

Preheat the oven to 200°C/180°C fan/400°F/ gas mark 6 and grease and line a 1 lb (450 g) loaf tin. Melt the butter then add it to a large mixing bowl with the buttermilk, milk, beaten egg and polenta. Mix and set aside for 10 minutes.

Fold in the grated cheese and then sift in the flour, baking powder and salt, folding in again until thoroughly combined. Pour into the tin and smooth the top with the back of a spoon. Bake for 35 minutes until golden. Cool in the tin for 10 minutes then turn out carefully onto a wire rack and leave until completely cool before slicing. You can freeze this and defrost slices for avocado toast for lunch.

Garlic bread

Shop-bought gluten-free garlic bread can be expensive and hard to come by. Instead, make your own flavoured garlic and herb butter to freeze and then spread on fresh bread and bake whenever you fancy it. The butter takes minutes to make and, once frozen, you can have garlic bread on the table to order in moments, too.

Makes 1 log of frozen garlic butter | Takes 5 minutes + baking the bread

INGREDIENTS

200 g (7 oz) butter, softened
2 cloves of garlic, crushed
2 big handfuls of flat-leaf parsley
a gluten-free baguette,
  to assemble
coarse sea salt, to assemble

METHOD

Beat the butter in a mixing bowl with a wooden spoon. Add the garlic and flat-leaf parsley and beat them in. Tip the butter mix onto a sheet of baking parchment. Roll the paper around the butter to form a log and twist the ends of the paper like a Christmas cracker. Store for up to 3 months in the freezer.

When you fancy garlic bread, preheat the oven to 240°C/220°C fan/475°F/gas mark 9. Slice off rounds of the frozen butter. Make deep cuts along the top of baguette every 2 cm (¾ in.) or so and add rounds of butter to each little pocket. Sprinkle with coarse sea salt. Bake until golden, melted and just beginning to char on the edges.

Focaccia

This delicious olive oil and rosemary-flavoured loaf is much simpler
to make than you might think. It is best enjoyed as soon as it's
cooled from the oven, drizzled with a little extra olive oil.

Makes 1 loaf | Takes 1 hour 10 minutes + cooling

INGREDIENTS

110 g (4 oz)
   gluten-free
   bread flour
220 g (8 oz)
   cornflour
55 g (2 oz) ground
   almonds
2 tsp salt
2 tsp xanthan gum
2 tsp sugar
2 heaped tsp
   gluten-free
   quick yeast
350 ml (12 fl oz)
   warm water
2 tbsp extra virgin
   olive oil, plus
   extra to serve
2 tsp rosemary,
   chopped
1 tsp sea salt flakes

METHOD

Grease a large baking tray with olive oil. Mix the flour, cornflour,
ground almonds, salt, xanthan gum, sugar and yeast in a large
mixing bowl.

Whisk the water and oil in a bowl. Add to dry ingredients, mixing
together with a wooden spoon. Beat for 2–3 minutes until dough
starts to thicken and begins to come away from the edges of
the bowl.

Turn out onto the tray and use a spatula to spread it into a round
loaf about 3 cm (1¼ in.) deep in the middle and 20 cm (8 in.) in
diameter. Don't worry that the dough is sloppy. Run the spatula
around the edges to neaten and smooth the top. Leave to rise
for 30 minutes draped with lightly oiled cling film. Towards the
end of proving, preheat the oven to 220°C/200°C fan/425°F/
gas mark 7.

Remove the cling film and with wet fingers, make little dimples in
the top of the dough. Scatter with the rosemary and salt, pushing
the rosemary into the dimples. Bake for 30 minutes until golden.
Leave to cool fully on a wire rack before slicing. To serve, drizzle
slices with extra olive oil.

Pretzels

The taste and texture of pretzels depends on getting the bicarbonate bath quantities right, as well as rolling the dough as per the instructions – so make sure you've read the method thoroughly before you start, and perhaps look at some step-by-step images online so you understand how to form the distinctive shapes. Once you learn how to make them, you'll realize that they're very easy – and delicious.

Makes 4 pretzels | Takes 45 minutes

INGREDIENTS

2 heaped tsp gluten-free quick yeast

1 tsp caster sugar

150 ml (5 fl oz) warm water

250 g (9 oz) gluten-free plain flour

1 tsp xanthan gum

1 tsp salt

2 tbsp bicarbonate of soda

1 egg, beaten

coarse sea salt or sesame seeds, for sprinkling

METHOD

Preheat the oven to 200°C/180°C fan/400°F/gas mark 6 and lightly oil a large baking sheet. Whisk together the yeast and sugar with the warm water. Put the flour, xanthan gum and salt in a food processor and add the yeast mix. Whizz in the food processor for 20–30 seconds until the dough just starts to form a rough ball.

Fill a large pan with 1.5 l (53 fl oz) of water, bring to the boil and add the bicarbonate of soda. While the large pan is heating up, decant the dough onto a worktop (you shouldn't need to flour it), knead for a minute then divide into 4 pieces. Knead each for 1 minute more until smooth then roll each piece by hand into a thin smooth rope about 45 cm (18 in.) long. Form pretzels by looping the ropes, twisting over at the ends and pressing down to seal (see above).

Using a wide spatula or fish slice to transfer the pretzels, dip each in the bicarbonate bath for 1 minute then remove and drain on a wire rack placed over a tea towel to catch any drips.

Place the pretzels on the baking sheet. Brush with beaten egg, sprinkle with coarse sea salt or sesame seeds and then bake for 15 minutes. Best enjoyed fresh from the oven.

Pizza muffins

These veggie-packed pizza muffins are lovely served warm. The muffins freeze well so you can make a batch and then take them out to thaw and reheat for a quick snack.

Makes 9 | Takes 35 minutes

INGREDIENTS

olive oil for greasing tin
2 eggs
100 ml (3½ fl oz) milk
50 g (2 oz) butter, melted
150 g (5 oz) self-raising
  gluten-free flour
1 tsp dried oregano
120 g (4½ oz) cheddar, grated
100 g (3½ oz) sweetcorn
3 spring onions, very finely sliced
30 g (1 oz) red pepper,
  deseeded and very finely diced

METHOD

Preheat the oven to 200°C/180°C fan/400°F/gas mark 6 and grease a muffin tin with a little olive oil.

Beat the eggs in a mixing bowl then add the milk and melted butter and mix together. Add the flour, oregano, cheddar, sweetcorn, spring onions and red pepper and mix everything to combine.

Divide the batter between 9 holes in the tin and bake for 25 minutes until golden. Gently pop out of the tin using a palette knife and eat warm from the oven or leave to cool on a wire rack.

Banana bread

Walnuts and chocolate chips elevate this banana bread into something really special. It has a super-crunchy coating and is fluffy and soft inside.

Makes 1 loaf | Takes 1 hour 15 minutes

INGREDIENTS

140 g (5 oz) unsalted
  butter, softened
250 g (9 oz) demerara sugar
2 ripe bananas, mashed
2 eggs
250 g (9 oz) gluten-free
  self-raising flour
1 tsp xanthan gum
100 g (3½ oz) walnuts,
  roughly chopped
100 g (3½ oz) gluten-free
  chocolate chips

METHOD

Preheat the oven to 200°C/180°C fan/400°F/gas mark 6 and grease and line a 1 lb (450 g) loaf tin. In a large mixing bowl, cream together the butter and the sugar with electric beaters. Add the mashed bananas and the eggs. Beat until combined. Sift the flour and xanthan gum into the bowl and beat again, then fold in the walnuts and chocolate chips with a spoon. Bake for 1 hour, checking on the bread at 45 minutes and if it is getting dark, covering the top loosely with foil.

After 1 hour, check if the loaf is cooked by inserting a skewer in the middle of the cake. If it comes out clean, it's cooked, if not, bake for another 10 minutes (bake times vary depending on the size of the bananas). Leave to cool in the tin for 10 minutes then turn out and leave to cool completely before slicing.

Victoria sponge

You can choose to leave the creamy filling in this cake oozing out (like the picture) or neaten it if you prefer by running a palette knife around the edges. Either way, the filling looks pretty if you marble the jam through the whipped cream a little bit when you add it.

Makes 1 cake | Takes 40 minutes

INGREDIENTS

345 g (12 oz) unsalted
  butter, softened
345 g (12 oz) caster sugar
2 tsp vanilla extract
6 eggs
345 g (12 oz) gluten-free
  self-raising flour
150 ml (5 fl oz) double cream
200 ml (7 fl oz) Greek yoghurt
strawberry jam or
  blueberry compote
icing sugar for dusting over

METHOD

Preheat the oven to 190°C/170°C fan/375°F/ gas mark 5 and grease and line the base of three shallow 20 cm (8 in.) cake tins. In a medium-sized bowl, cream the butter, sugar and vanilla extract with electric beaters until pale and fluffy. Beat in the eggs, two at a time. Then sift in the flour, fold in a little and mix until thoroughly combined.

Divide evenly between the cake tins. Spread out in an even layer using a spatula and bake for 20 minutes until risen and golden. Cool in the tins for 5 minutes then turn out onto wire racks to cool completely.

Whip the cream until thick (stiff peak) with electric beaters then fold in the yoghurt. Use to sandwich the cake with layers of jam or compote, marbling the jam a little into the cream. Dust lightly with icing sugar to finish.

Cupcakes

You can colour the lemony frosting for these cupcakes any colour you like (or just leave plain). Add any additional sprinkles you fancy too but do read the labels as not all cupcake sprinkles are gluten-free.

Makes 12 | Takes 45 minutes plus cooling

CAKE INGREDIENTS

175 g (6 oz) unsalted butter, softened
175 g (6 oz) caster sugar
3 medium eggs
175 g (6 oz) self-raising gluten-free flour

FROSTING INGREDIENTS

225 g (8 oz) unsalted butter, softened
400 g (14 oz) icing sugar, sifted
1 lemon, juiced
food colouring (optional)

METHOD

Preheat the oven to 180°C/160°C fan/350°F/ gas mark 4 and line a 12-hole muffin tray with paper cases. Measure the butter and sugar into a large mixing bowl. Cream together until fluffy using electric beaters. Add the eggs one at a time, beating in after each addition until smooth. Sift the flour into the bowl and fold in. Spoon into the paper cases and bake for 20 minutes. Leave to cool on a wire rack.

While the cakes are cooling, make the frosting. Beat the butter in a medium-sized bowl with electric beaters then gradually add the icing sugar and lemon juice plus a few drops of food colouring, if desired. Once the cakes are cool, ice them by spooning or piping on the frosting.

Little carrot cakes

Use a food processor to effortlessly grate the carrots for these fluffy, delicately spiced little cakes. Add a little honey to the reduced-sugar, cream cheese frosting to achieve the sweetness of standard icing sugar.

Makes 6 | Takes 40 minutes

CAKE INGREDIENTS

125 g (4½ oz) carrots (about 1 large one)

75 g (3 oz) unsalted butter, softened

100 g (3½ oz) golden caster sugar

1 egg

100 g (3½ oz) gluten-free brown rice flour

1 tsp gluten-free baking powder

½ tsp cinnamon

60 g (2 oz) sultanas

FROSTING INGREDIENTS

165 g (6 oz) cream cheese

3 tsp of honey

6 pecan nuts, to decorate

METHOD

Preheat the oven to 200°C/180°C fan/400°F/gas mark 6 and line a muffin tray with six paper cases. Peel and grate the carrots (a food processor with a grater attachment makes short work of this).

Measure the butter and sugar into a large mixing bowl. Cream together until fluffy using electric beaters. Add the egg and beat again. Sift in the flour, baking powder and cinnamon and beat these in too. Add the grated carrot and sultanas and stir in until fully combined. Divide the mixture between the muffin cases, bake for 15–20 minutes until golden then cool on a wire rack.

While the cakes are cooling, make the frosting. Beat together the cream cheese and honey with electric beaters. Once the cakes are cool, ice them by spooning on the frosting and topping each with a whole pecan. Best eaten the same day if iced or keep un-iced in a tin for a day or two.

Lemon drizzle cake

Polenta and ground almonds are gluten-free baking staples, providing bite to this fluffy cake and keeping it lovely and moist. The lemony, syrupy pistachio nuts on top make it extra special.

Makes 1 cake | Takes 1 hour 10 minutes

CAKE INGREDIENTS

175 g (6 oz) gluten-free self-raising flour

1½ tsp gluten-free baking powder

50 g (2 oz) ground almonds

50 g (2 oz) polenta

2 lemons, zested

140 g (5 oz) golden caster sugar

2 eggs

225 g (8 oz) natural yoghurt

75 ml (3 fl oz) rapeseed oil

FOR THE TOPPING

60 g (2 oz) caster sugar

2 lemons, juiced

50 g (2 oz) pistachios, chopped

METHOD

Preheat the oven to 180°C/160°C fan/350°F/gas mark 4 and grease and line a deep 20 cm (8 in.) round cake tin. Put the flour, baking powder, ground almonds, polenta, lemon zest and golden caster sugar in a bowl (keep the lemons to juice for the topping). Beat the eggs together with the yoghurt until smooth and add to the dry ingredients with the rapeseed oil. Fold everything together. Spoon into the tin, level off with a spoon and bake for 35–40 minutes. If it is looking a little brown in the final 10 minutes you can cover it loosely with foil.

Towards the end of baking, make the topping by heating the caster sugar and lemon juice in a saucepan over a low heat. Once the sugar is dissolved, remove from the heat and stir in the chopped pistachios.

Cool the cake for 15 minutes in the tin then remove from the tin and sit on a wire rack set over a baking tray (to catch any drips). Poke holes in the surface of the cake with a fork or skewer then spoon over the nut syrup, letting it soak in a little between additions. Leave to cool completely before slicing.

Double-decker chocolate cake

This richly iced chocolate cake is light and fluffy with the perfect quantity of chocolate frosting to sandwich it together and top. Add candles and different decorations to make any birthday special, switching out the hazelnuts for sprinkles if you prefer (beware: not all cake sprinkles are gluten-free).

Makes 1 cake | Takes 1 hour

CAKE INGREDIENTS

225 g (8 oz) unsalted butter, softened, plus extra for the tins
225 g (8 oz) caster sugar
4 eggs, beaten
225 g (8 oz) gluten-free self-raising flour
1 tsp gluten-free baking powder
2 tbsp cocoa powder
a pinch of salt
1 tbsp brewed coffee

FROSTING INGREDIENTS

140 g (5 oz) unsalted butter, softened
300 g (11 oz) icing sugar, sifted
4 tbsp cocoa powder, sifted
6 tbsp milk
25 g (1 oz) chopped roasted hazelnuts, to decorate (or use sprinkles)

METHOD

Preheat the oven to 180°C/160°C fan/350°F/ gas mark 4. Grease and line two shallow 20-cm (8-in.) non-stick sponge cake tins. Cream the butter and sugar with electric beaters until fluffy. Add the eggs gradually, beating after each addition.

Sift in the flour, baking powder, cocoa and a pinch of salt then add the coffee. Stir them in a bit by hand then mix in thoroughly with the beaters. Divide between the tins, spreading the batter out evenly. Bake for 20 minutes in the centre of the oven until spongy to the touch. Leave to cool in the tins for 10 minutes then transfer to a wire rack and cool completely before icing.

For the frosting, beat together the butter and half the icing sugar. Add the rest of the icing sugar, the cocoa and milk and beat again to form a frosting. Use to sandwich the cooled cake, and top with the remaining icing and the chopped hazelnuts (or other sprinkles).

Gingernut biscuits

You can freeze these gingernuts unbaked as the mixture makes plenty – a good way to ensure you always have gluten-free biscuits to hand. Just cook from frozen for 18 minutes in an oven preheated to 180°C/160°C fan/350°F/gas mark 4.

Makes 30 | Takes 35 minutes plus chilling

INGREDIENTS

300 g (11 oz) gluten-free plain flour
1 tsp gluten-free baking powder
½ tsp bicarbonate of soda
2 tsp ground ginger
½ tsp salt
200 g (7 oz) unsalted butter, chopped
300 g (11 oz) soft brown sugar
1 egg

METHOD

Stir the flour, baking powder, bicarbonate of soda, ginger and salt together in a large mixing bowl. Melt the butter and sugar together in a pan, then, with a wooden spoon, beat the egg in and then add to the dry ingredients, beating together to combine. Scrape down the edges of the bowl so that the mixture comes roughly together and then chill in the bowl for at least 2 hours in the fridge.

Get the dough out of the fridge for 10 minutes to warm up. Preheat the oven to 180°C/160°C fan/ 350°F/gas mark 4 and line two large baking trays with parchment. Roll the dough by hand into 30 balls (about the size of a walnut) and pop on the prepared trays, leaving plenty of room as they spread. Bake for 15 minutes until golden and cracked. Cool for 5 minutes on the trays then transfer to a wire rack to cool completely.

Chocolate chip hazelnut frozen cookie dough

With a bit of advance prep, you can have these brilliant cookies, loaded with chocolate chips and hazelnuts, whenever you want them. The recipe makes two large logs of dough so you can prep once in bulk and keep stashes of frozen dough on standby to bake in whatever quantities you fancy.

Makes 30 | Takes 15 minutes + freezing/baking

INGREDIENTS

275 g (10 oz) unsalted butter, softened

500 g (18 oz) light brown soft sugar

2 eggs

1 tbsp vanilla extract

475 g (17 oz) gluten-free rice flour

2 tsp gluten-free baking powder

150 g (5 oz) gluten-free chocolate chips

150 g (5 oz) hazelnuts, chopped

a pinch of salt

METHOD

Cream together the butter and sugar in a large mixing bowl using electric beaters. Add the eggs, beating in each until combined then whisk in the vanilla.

Sift in the flour and baking powder and whisk in until fully combined and stiff. Stir in the chocolate chips, nuts and salt.

Divide the dough in half and place each half on a large sheet of baking parchment. Shape each half into a log and roll up in the parchment, tying the ends with string, then freeze.

Once ready to cook, preheat the oven to 180°C/160°C fan/350°F/gas mark 4 and get the dough out of the freezer to rest for a few minutes. Line a baking sheet with parchment. Slice the dough into discs (make sure you remove all the parchment!). Transfer to the baking sheet leaving room as they spread. If the discs crumble, just squeeze the dough roughly back together – they'll bind and form cookies as they bake. Make as many as you want, storing the remaining dough in the freezer for another day. Bake for 15 minutes. Harden on the tray for a few minutes then transfer to a wire rack to cool (or eat warm).

Coffee cake

This classic cake is very easy to make and super-light and fluffy. The coffee frosting is pretty addictive.

Makes 1 cake | Takes 45 minutes + cooling

CAKE INGREDIENTS

225 g (8 oz) unsalted
  butter, softened

225 g (8 oz) caster sugar

4 eggs, beaten

225 g (8 oz) gluten-free
  self-raising flour

1 tsp gluten-free baking powder

3 tbsp coffee

FROSTING INGREDIENTS

140 g (5 oz) unsalted
  butter, softened

300 g (11 oz) icing sugar, sifted

3 tbsp coffee

25 g (1 oz) walnuts, chopped

METHOD

Preheat the oven to 180°C/160°C fan/350°F/ gas mark 4 and grease and line two shallow 20-cm (8-in.) non-stick cake tins. Beat the butter and sugar together with electric beaters until pale and fluffy. Beat in the eggs a little at a time until combined. Sift in the flour and baking powder then add the coffee to the bowl. Stir everything in a bit by hand then mix in thoroughly with the beaters (stirring first prevents flour exploding everywhere).

Divide between the tins and bake for 20 minutes. Leave to cool in the tins for 10 minutes then transfer to a wire rack and cool completely before icing.

To make the frosting, use electric beaters to mix together the butter with half the icing sugar until smooth (this takes several minutes). Add the rest of the icing sugar together with the coffee and beat together again to form a glossy frosting. Use to sandwich and ice the cooled cake and top with the chopped walnuts.

Brownies

This recipe makes brownies how they should be: intense and fudgy, slightly chewy around the edges and crackly on top. You can leave out the nuts altogether to make a plain version.

Makes 16 | Takes 40 minutes

INGREDIENTS

- 100 g (3½ oz) gluten-free dark chocolate, broken into chunks
- 100 g (3½ oz) gluten-free milk chocolate, broken into chunks
- 250 g (9 oz) unsalted butter
- 400 g (14 oz) soft dark brown sugar
- 4 eggs
- 140 g (5 oz) gluten-free plain flour
- 50 g (2 oz) cocoa powder
- 150 g (5 oz) macadamia nuts (or blanched hazelnuts), roughly chopped (optional)

METHOD

Preheat the oven to 180°C/160°C fan/350°F/gas mark 4. Line a 20-cm x 20-cm (8-in. x 8-in.) baking tin with parchment. In a large saucepan, gently melt the chocolate, butter and sugar over a low heat, stirring occasionally until melted. Remove from the heat and leave to cool for a few minutes.

Add the eggs and beat together in the pan with a wooden spoon until glossy and fully combined. Fold in the flour, cocoa powder and nuts (if using) and incorporate fully. Pour the mix into the prepared tin and bake for 50 minutes. Cool completely in the tin then slice into squares with a sharp knife on a board.

Scones

These scones are at their most moreish while still warm from the oven, but you can bake them and then cool to eat later the same day. Either way, don't skimp on jam and butter.

Makes 6 | Takes 30 minutes

INGREDIENTS

225 g (8 oz) gluten-free self-raising flour, plus some extra aside

½ tsp salt

55 g (2 oz) unsalted butter, diced

150 ml (5 fl oz) milk, plus a little extra for glazing

blueberry or strawberry jam and butter, to serve

METHOD

Preheat the oven to 220°C/200°C fan/425°F/gas mark 7. Flour a baking sheet. Sift the flour and salt into a large mixing bowl. Rub in the butter until the mixture resembles breadcrumbs. Make a well in the crumbs and pour in the milk. Mix to a dough using a palette knife.

On a floured worktop, knead very lightly until just smooth. Roll or press out the dough until it's about 2.5 cm (1 in.) thick and stamp out rounds with a small pastry cutter that has been dipped in flour. For even scones, pull the cutter up without twisting it and transfer each to your prepped baking sheet. Gently re-roll the remaining dough and repeat until you've used it all. Brush the scones with a little more milk. Bake for 15 minutes. Serve warm from the oven, spread with jam and butter (or cool on a wire rack to eat later the same day).

Gingerbread men

Everybody's favourite Christmas recipe, only gluten-free. The biscuits firm up on the tray once out of the oven. Try baking for 8 minutes for a softer biscuit or 10 minutes for one with more snap.

Makes 10 | Takes 30 minutes + chilling

INGREDIENTS

115 g (4 oz) gluten-free plain flour, plus extra for rolling out

a pinch of bicarbonate of soda

2 tsp ground ginger

1 tsp mixed spice

30 g (1 oz) unsalted butter

50 g (2 oz) light brown soft sugar

2 tbsp runny honey

a little icing sugar, mixed with a few drops of water until pipeable

METHOD

Mix the flour, bicarbonate of soda and spices in a bowl. Melt the butter, sugar and honey together in a pan over a low heat. Once the sugar is dissolved, pour the wet mix into the dry mix and combine to make a soft dough. Wrap in cling film and chill for 1 hour.

Preheat the oven to 200°C/180°C fan/400°F/ gas mark 6 and line a large baking sheet with parchment. Roll out the dough on a floured surface to 3 mm (⅛ in.) thick. Cut out gingerbread men and transfer to the prepared baking sheet. Bake for 8–10 minutes until golden. While still warm, make eyes, mouths and buttons in the gingerbread men with a cocktail stick or skewer. Harden on the tray then transfer to a wire rack. Cool completely before icing with boots or scarves.

Easy cheesecake pots

These delicious little desserts are like individual servings of gluten-free strawberry cheesecake. They're very easy to assemble — and eat.

Makes 4 | Taks 10 minutes plus chilling

INGREDIENTS

150 ml (5 fl oz) double cream

200 ml (7 fl oz) Greek yoghurt

1 lime, zested and juiced

1 tbsp honey

4 gingernut biscuits (see p.138 or use gluten-free shop-bought)

a handful of strawberries, hulled and sliced

METHOD

Whip the cream to soft peaks with electric beaters then fold in the yoghurt, the lime zest and juice, plus the honey. Blitz the biscuits to fine crumbs in a food processor then divide between four glasses, pressing down the biscuit layer firmly with a spoon. Top with the cream mixture then a few sliced strawberries. Chill for at least half an hour before serving.

Ice cream waffle sandwiches

It's not always easy to get hold of gluten-free waffle cones – and chocolate flake cones tend not to be gluten-free, either. This recipe is designed to fulfil the role instead. You'll need a mini, inexpensive, round waffle iron to make them. Look for one that's 12 cm (5 in.) in diameter. This is because most leading brands of ice cream sold in small round tubs are 12 cm (5 in.) in diameter too, making it really easy to slice rounds of ice cream to match the waffles.

Makes 5 | Takes 25 minutes plus freezing

INGREDIENTS

40 g (1½ oz)
 unsalted butter

125 g (4½ oz)
 gluten-free
 self-raising flour

1 tbsp caster sugar

175 ml (6 fl oz) milk

1 egg

100 g (3½ oz)
 gluten-free
 chocolate chips

gluten-free vanilla
 ice cream

a handful of
 gluten-free
 sprinkles

METHOD

Begin heating the waffle iron. Meanwhile, melt the butter. Combine the flour and sugar in a medium-sized mixing bowl. Whisk together the milk, melted butter and egg then pour into the dry ingredients and whisk again to form a smooth batter. Cook 10 waffles according to manufacturer's instructions. Leave to cool. Meanwhile melt the chocolate chips gently in a bain-marie.

Use baking parchment to line a baking sheet that will fit in your freezer. Once you have all your waffles ready, take the ice cream out of the freezer and get a chopping board out. Use a sharp knife to slice off a round of ice cream, right through the paper packaging. Peel off the paper and sandwich together two waffles with the ice cream disc. Repeat to make all the sandwiches. Drizzle or spread melted chocolate over each one, top with sprinkles and freeze again until needed (or the chocolate is set).

Conclusion

The recipes in this collection are intended to be easy, accessible and just a small taste of the dishes you can cook up in your gluten-free kitchen. Remember, it takes a while to adapt to any new diet and way of cooking, so be kind to yourself and take small steps along your new journey of eating without gluten. You don't have to start baking perfect gluten-free bread the day after you're diagnosed as coeliac.

As your body begins to recover, you'll feel more and more encouraged to get into the kitchen and whip up new dishes that not only taste great but make you feel better, too.

Try to be organized and plan ahead whenever possible. By either packing your own food or establishing in advance where you can eat out gluten-free, you'll avoid ending up stressed, hungry and having to improvise on the go. Similarly, stocking your cupboards, fridge and freezer with standbys and staples means that, more often than not, you'll have a quick fix to come home to and make for dinner without having to rush around trying to find last-minute gluten-free ingredients. It's also good for your bank balance. The planner on p.18 can help you.

Remember you don't have to change everything all at once. In time you'll find a new rhythm, prepping ahead and batch cooking when you have the time, while relying on short cuts and easy-cook ideas on days when you don't.

Meanwhile, there's a whole new world of gluten-free food to discover that both tastes great and makes you feel better. And that's definitely something to celebrate.

About the author

Emily Kerrigan is a registered nutritionist and food writer. When her daughter was diagnosed with coeliac disease, she studied for a master's degree in nutrition and completed a Leiths Cookery School diploma to boot. Emily combines her years working on food magazines with her first-class nutrition knowledge to create deliciously nourishing gluten-free food for everyday eating. Her recipes are fresh, fuss-free and reliable and she thinks, in a balanced diet, there's room for both greens and gluten-free chocolate.

Index

VEGAN SNACKS

SIMPLE, DELICIOUS SWEET AND SAVOURY TREATS

Elanor Clarke
Hardback
978-1-78685-970-9

Welcome to a delicious world of vegan nibbles

From the healthy to the decadent, from on-the-go breakfast ideas to after-dinner indulgences, this book has sweet bites and savoury treats to satisfy everyone.
Try not to swoon as you whip up delights such as:

- tofu poké bowl
- matcha tea and lime pie
- jackfruit tacos
- apple pie milkshake
- pitta pizza
- chocolate chip cookie dough
- buffalo cauli wings

Whether you have only a few minutes to prepare a quick morsel or you want to create something truly impressive to satisfy those cravings, these tasty recipes are all you need to keep your hunger pangs at bay.

THE PLANET-FRIENDLY KITCHEN

HOW TO SHOP AND COOK WITH A CONSCIENCE

Karen Edwards
Hardback
978-1-78783-691-4

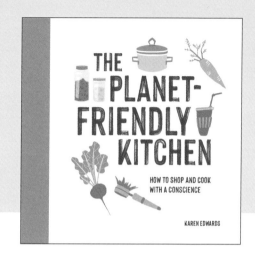

We all have the power to make a difference

We know our planet's resources are stretched to the limits. We know that without significant changes to our diets and shopping habits, nature will continue to suffer. But sometimes it feels like we're bombarded with mixed messages, and it can be hard to work out which foods are truly eco-friendly. This book sets out the facts in a clear and straightforward way, helping you to make informed choices about environmentally conscious ways to shop, the products to avoid, the best foods to buy, and sustainable ways to prepare them.

With over 30 delicious recipes that you, and the earth, will love, *The Planet-Friendly Kitchen* contains all the tips and advice you need to start making small changes that have big impacts. The choices we make can help create a kinder way of feeding the world, and will preserve our beautiful planet for many generations to come.

Have you enjoyed this book?

If so, find us on Facebook at SUMMERSDALE PUBLISHERS, on Twitter/X at @SUMMERSDALE and on Instagram and TikTok at @SUMMERSDALEBOOKS and get in touch. We'd love to hear from you!

WWW.SUMMERSDALE.COM